DIGGING FOR GOLD

EMMANUEL ELENDU

WestBow®
PRESS
A DIVISION OF THOMAS NELSON
& ZONDERVAN

Unless otherwise noted, all Scripture quotations are from the New King James version of the Bible. Copyright © 1979, 1980, 1982 by Thomas Nelson, Inc., publishers Used by permission

Scripture taken from the New King James Version. Copyright © 1979, 1980, 1982 by Thomas Nelson, Inc. Used by permission. All rights reserved.

WestBow Press books may be ordered through booksellers or by contacting:

WestBow Press
A Division of Thomas Nelson & Zondervan
1663 Liberty Drive
Bloomington, IN 47403
www.westbowpress.com
1 (866) 928-1240

Because of the dynamic nature of the Internet, any web addresses or links contained in this book may have changed since publication and may no longer be valid. The views expressed in this work are solely those of the author and do not necessarily reflect the views of the publisher, and the publisher hereby disclaims any responsibility for them.

Any people depicted in stock imagery provided by Thinkstock are models, and such images are being used for illustrative purposes only. Certain stock imagery © Thinkstock.

ISBN: 978-1-4908-7956-7 (sc)
ISBN: 978-1-4908-7958-1 (hc)
ISBN: 978-1-4908-7957-4 (e)

Library of Congress Control Number: 2015907612

Print information available on the last page.

WestBow Press rev. date: 05/27/2015

"Masterfully craft your salvation with deep and undivided attention to details as you embrace grace, mercy, and wisdom."

Dedicated to the faithful, the servants of the Lord Jesus Christ who hold the truth in righteousness and to the few who study, teach, and live by the Word, even today

CONTENTS

ACKNOWLEDGMENTS

In compiling these studies, many disciples spent valuable time and resources toward the completion of this book. I do not have the luxury of space here to recognize all the generals who, through prayers and support, helped with this work. The following, however, need be mentioned for their great contributions:

Pastor Mrs. Chinwe Elendu, my beloved wife and mother of our two young men and woman (Samuel, David, and Ruth). She prayed life into this project. She also is the pastor in charge of Children's and Teens Church at Dominion Center. This work would not be possible without her having stayed the course and providing encouragement at the most needed moments of my ministry challenges. God bless my wife!

Brother Gbile Akanni, Reverend Charles Achonwa; Reverend Chris Okeke, who the Lord used to make indelible marks on my spiritual growth; I will not forget their years of discipleship and mentoring. Thank you!

Dr. Patrick Anyalewechi of the Church of the Nazarene, West Chester, Ohio, is worthy of mention. He read through my manuscripts and made very studious corrections. He advised me as many times as I went to him for counsel. He is a gift to the body of Christ and to me; a professor of psychology and behavioral sciences at Wilberforce University, Wilberforce, Ohio.

Mrs. Nkechi Azuka, a professor of social work at Nyack College (Alliance Theological Institute in the School of Counseling). She also is a licensed master social worker (NY, NJ and OH), clinician, and psychotherapist. She helped with proofreading and corrections. Nkechi is indeed a blessing to those who know her and what she brings to the table. She read through the original script.

Thank you to all the members of RCCG Dominion Center in Cincinnati and Dayton, Ohio, and northern Kentucky, as well as the elders and their pastors. They have been a source of encouragement and support through these years of work. May the Lord continue to nurture you all in the most holy faith.

Some organizations have been a part of the work in Dominion Center. They include Wilson Memorial Hospital, Sidney, Ohio; West Chester Hospital (an arm of University of Cincinnati Health); Hope Word Church; Tryed Stone New Beginning Church; and a handful of others. Thank you for your kindness, fellowship, and gifts.

Very important are those who helped during periods of financial crunch. Dr. Charles Azuka, Pastor Nosa Idahosa, Dr. Abraham Chukwu, Dr. Henry Okafor, Dr. Chinedu Njoku, Eze (Barrister) Julius Emetu and Tony Onuorah (who provided shelter), and Patrick Olabode, who paid my transport fare "to go start the work" in Cincinnati in 2002. Dr. Kunle Oyekanmi, my faithful and dependable assistant pastor, Dr. Ayodele Adebayo, Dr. Arinze Ikeme, Dr. Yemi Ajayi; to mention a few. May the Lord bless you all, and please continue the good work.

Last, but the most important, I owe the Lord and His Holy Spirit all the worship and gratitude for the insight and wisdom to put together this little piece of work. To you, Lord Jesus, be all honor and glory forever. Amen!

INTRODUCTION

Digging for Gold

Digging for gold is no simple job to undertake. As herculean as that may be, mining and extraction and then purification of gold are tasks that speak volumes to the value investors place on this liquid metal. I had the opportunity to discuss this process with Richmond Cole, one of our brothers in Dominion Center who has witnessed how gold is extracted and mined in Ghana. It was thrilling and enriching to know that gold acquisition and the labor around it is not meant for feeble minds. Digging for gold must be thought out thoroughly and well planned. Cole's description prompted me to research how gold is processed, as I was going to submit a piece of the Lord's instructions to me under the title "Digging for Gold." Of course, the title is an allegory of a search for something of more value than gold, something that dives deeply into the supernatural to obtain and "own" the essence of living. I was quick to flip to the web's Wikipedia to validate my story.

We seek much more than gold. We seek and walk toward obtaining the heavenly kingdom, where the streets are made of gold, where we have many mansions (rooms) for everyone who submits and lives the life exemplified in Christ Jesus, where there is no night or day because the light, the groom, is always there shining to His bride forever. The Father's unbending resolve to give us the kingdom and call us to His bosom quells all strife and lends answers to all questions regarding this truth.

Once delivered from the kingdom of darkness into the kingdom of His dear Son, it is our responsibility to learn and discover how to grow from babies to fully mature adults so that the inheritance and the government of His kingdom can be bequeathed to us. Kingdom life requires kingdom principles. There are set rules and order. Beyond the walls of a church, Jesus is teaching order—rules and character that people of the kingdom must possess and live by. The writings in this book are not academic or a show of prose; they are instructions the Father gave to me through revelations at different times. I have selected to address some issues in the hope that these topics will act as stimuli to you to further "demystify" the Scriptures and bring to the church a wider coverage and expanded reach.

This book is a study book, with many questions that you need to answer. To get the most from the book, I suggest that you organize a small Bible study group in your church, home, or workplace. Intelligently discuss the issues of our contemporary society, relate them to Scriptures, and come up with action items (things to do) about what you have learned. Prayer is very important to fully appreciate the flow in this study. I commend you to the Lord, who is able to reveal to you the secret things of the kingdom through this book.

Any time you feel left behind or confused, do not hesitate to ask your mentor or pastor for help. You also can send an email to me at emmaelendu@yahoo.com. God bless you, and have fun as you study.

...Emmanuel Elendu

CHAPTER 1

Taking Dominion Over All Things

You made a decision to follow and serve the Lord Jesus, possibly years ago, but now, the momentum may be gone. The zeal and desire to serve the love of your life may be diminished and faded to the point that you can barely tell the sheep from the goat.

I can hear you groaning; it is not uncommon to bask in nostalgia about the events of the years behind you. Your current situation has not diminished the passion and desire for God in your life, but there seems to be a drought of grace—you did everything possible to come out on top but the condition of your life, at this moment, might scare observers. Yes, you did your best, but fortune and destiny seem a million miles away.

You prayed, fasted, and even gave alms. It just did not work out the way you planned. You tell yourself that it is time to change your strategy and try another method—to go the way of Egypt and catch up with your pals. Do not go down to Egypt; stay here. Read this book. You are about to unlock the door of spiritual revival and unprecedented blessing from the love of your life, the God of your salvation.

> And there was a famine in the land, beside the first famine that was in the days of Abraham. And Isaac went unto Abimelech, king of the Philistines unto Gera. And the Lord appeared unto him and said, "Go not down into Egypt; dwell in the land which I shall tell thee of: sojourn

1

in this land and I will be with thee and will bless thee; for unto thee and thy seed will I give all these countries and I will perform the oath which I swore unto Abraham thy father. I will make thy seed to multiply as the stars of heaven and I will give unto thy seed all these countries; and in thy seed shall all the nations of the earth be blessed; because that Abraham obeyed my voice and kept my charge, my commandments, my statues and my laws." And Isaac dwelt in Gera. (Genesis 26:1–6 KJV)

Children of the covenant live under the cover of that covenant. As a child of the covenant, God has paved a path for you. He takes responsibility for it and pursues His purpose and plan for your life until they come to fruition. I want to encourage you to learn of Him. "My yoke is easy, my burden is light," Jesus said. The trip to heaven is for champions and for the mature. It is for those who will have dominion over their circumstances and situations.

My passion is to guide you through strategic positioning in the things of God and your vocation as you set sail in life. As we study, please dare to live in dominion in the kingdom. I invite you into the family of God, in the kingdom where God rules. If you can agree with Him, you'll be a part of the kingdom. It's more than just a church thing. It goes beyond your ethnicity or profession. It draws its lifeline in God. The Holy Spirit empowers this principle and employs the expression of the kingdom lifestyle in you. You are welcome on board. Bon voyage!

Beaten But Not Down
2 Corinthians 4:1–7

You must forget the past, though history can be a useful tool in learning and fostering a purposeful and strategic position. Yet to live with the failures of yesterday is both dangerous and demeaning to your soul and psyche. The past is gone. Should the failures and unaccomplished dreams of your past go with it? Remember: though you fall seven times, yet will you rise again. Paul did his best under God, but some of his audience was so antagonistic, refusing to accept his apostleship, that he despaired of life. Death worked in him, but life worked in his antagonists. As he preached peace and encouragement to others, he was suffering, weak, and run down. Encourage yourself in the Lord, and take up your mantle again.

Read Psalm 27:4-14; 1Peter 2:21-25; Isaiah 43:1-7; Psalm 28:6-9

There are spiritual "pills" you must take to overcome defeat:
1. Receive mercy, grace, and truth. Let the Lord into your heart. Cooperate with and obey Him!
2. Follow in His steps and rejoice over your circumstance. Sing for joy, for your day of remembrance is here. Count yourself privileged to suffer for His sake and move on to a higher realm with God.
3. Do not let fear grip your soul. The Devil you saw in the past will be gone forever. *Fear not!*
4. Cheer up. God is able to do much more than you can imagine. The lesson of yesterday that you must learn is as follows: Though death supposedly worked in you as life filled everywhere else, there was a purpose. That purpose is so that you might know that the excellence of the power, grace, and favor, which will be released a short time from now, is of God and not of you. It has been held back because God insists that no flesh may glory in His presence. In other words, God is waiting for a prepared you before He releases the bounties of heaven for you. Be prepared; be a disciple; mature; and gird your lions for the pack.

Set Yourself on the Watch
Habakkuk 2:1–3; Psalm 37:1–25

"I will stand upon my watch, and set me upon the tower and will watch to see what He will say unto me and what I shall answer when I am reproved" (Habakkuk 2:1KJV).

To wallow in darkness or plunge into life or ministry without direction and purpose is a dangerous venture. Because the Lord wants us to be guided and instructed (Psalm 38:8–10), He reveals His mind concerning every situation. He promises that you will never be forsaken (Psalm 37:25), so He demands that you wait on Him. To wait is to set time when and where you can hear Him speak to you. No commander sends a soldier to the warfront without adequate preparation and training. You must go back to Him to be instructed on strategies and methods of how to go about your Christian life. Go on a retreat. Fast and pray. Study the Word, and listen to the voice of the Holy Spirit. Get out of the crowd. Set yourself on a watch. Do everything you can to hear and get direction from God. *Do it now!*

To-Do List

1. Receive divine mandate and instructions.

   Dwell in the land. Don't quit (Luke 19:12–13; Genesis 26:1–3).

   Delight yourself in the Lord (Psalm 27:4; Psalm 37).

   Be calm and patient. Wait on the Lord, for He shall surely speak (Amos 3:7; Hebrews 10:37–41).

2. Rebuild your ban for the new harvest.

   Strategize and sequence your operations (Luke 10:1–8; 22:35–37).

   Supply in-put resources to execute your project (Proverbs 6:1–6; Luke 19:10–13)

   Strengthen yourself.

   Enlarge the place; lengthen the cords and straighten the stakes (Isaiah 54:1–8)

3. Enter into a covenant with God.

   Build an altar as a memorial to God—self and family altars (Genesis 28; Joshua 4:1–14).

Do not clench your fist. *Give* unto the Lord. *Pay your tithes* and offer *quality offerings* to the Lord (Proverbs 11:22–24; Malachi 3:7–10; 2 Corinthians 8; 9).

Invest your harvest. Choose a good portfolio, after counsel and much prayer. Make sure you do not eat your seed from the harvest. Do not keep company with consumers who do not think about the next investment opportunity. Think about David and his sacrificial giving and of Hannah's covenant with God as she prayed for Samuel and how she honored the Lord in fulfilling her promise. May the Lord depend on you to be faithful. Amen.

Partnering with God
Hebrews 5:12–14

Armed with the knowledge that the end of all things is near, and with the passion to do the will of our God, we come to the point where any business or venture in which we engage without enlisting God as the principle partner is fruitless and ephemeral. It is not sustainable. We must be anointed. To belittle working for the Lord is to play the fool. Working for the Master is not limited to pastors and bishops or your Sunday school teacher; it goes as far as medical doctors, lawyers, nurses and nursing assistants, social workers, teachers, businessmen—whatever you are. You must find use in the hand and house of God (2 Timothy 2:19–21). That is the only way to stay fervent and keep your relevance, spiritually. Ask yourself and the Lord these questions:

- Lord, what would you have me do in your kingdom, starting with your church?
- What is my share of the assignment to prepare men for your second coming?
- How do I start, and what tools or spiritual and material resources are there to assess the work?

Get a blueprint of what to do—specific plans and projects for the family and your church and community—and then drill down to individuals in the family and departments in the church and farther in areas in which you may be skilled to affect your community.

Family Church

Another component of the partnership with God is to discover your niche in God's fivefold ministry—your calling and your ministry. Ephesians 4:11–14 outlines them succinctly: apostles, prophets, evangelists, pastors, and teachers.

Added to the list above are helpers, governments, and administration offices you can fill in His church. The idea is that "Until we all come in the unity of the faith, and of the knowledge of the Son of God, unto the measure of the stature of the fullness of Christ" (Ephesians 4:13).

And God's ultimate goal for all these engagements is that we no longer will remain babies but be mature and ready to run with the message of our Lord Jesus Christ:

"That henceforth be no more children, tossed to and fro, and carried about with every wind of doctrine, by the sleight of men, and cunning craftiness, whereby they lie in wait to deceive" (Ephesians 4:14).

Do you know why you should not be forced to go to church and enlist in the workforce of God? Do you know why you should stay at your duty post and be consistent and purposeful with one local congregation (except in a case of apostasy)? Those who flicker and spin around are babies and need to mature.

Devotional

1. Assuming God has promised me only one year to live on earth, how would that affect my attitude to life?
2. In a partnership business, equity and liabilities are shared, according to resources put in the business. Equity/debt ratio: how much weight (ratio) is my contribution? To what extent can God

trust my commitment in this deal? What do I expect in return when we close the books?

3. Discuss this eternal business with your spouse. Come up with a project from your understanding of this study, please. Meet with your pastor or bishop for guidance in execution.

A Disciple like His Master

"If anyone comes to Me and does not hate his father and mother, wife and children, brothers and sisters, yes and his own life also, he cannot be My disciple ... so likewise whoever of you does not forsake all that he has cannot be My disciple" (Luke 14:26, 33). Please consider this friendly piece of advice from a real life event, and learn from the experience of others: Here's what happened:

He stood with a look of importance. The masterful architecture that his church employed told me that my friend had come a long way through the hue and cry of corporate life. His clothing was Italian in design and looked regal. No comments were needed about the set of golden wares and decorations at the altar. His crew from the Episcopal Church were a no-nonsense group, equipped with the armor and power to dismantle both men and spirits in their quest to conquer and rule, especially here on earth.

I stood speechless, waiting to gather my share of the Word of Life. The colors, the displays, and echo of voices seemed shrill in contrast to the purpose of my visit. As thousands echoed, "Hallelujah! Amen," it seemed that the heavens would fall when the real stuff was declared. And lo, hearts and lives waiting for the food remained starved, as they were wary of the excited man in the pulpit. It seemed to me that he hurried to the pulpit that morning. I think he made it to the ministry (or to profession of preaching) sooner than he became a Christian.

As I watched, I saw frustration—a lack of passage and a shrink from the Spirit of grace. It was everything, shy of the fire, that every believer expected from the pulpit. His semantics were superb; his colors and matching displays, along with the money talks, were supremely entertaining. But I knew hungry souls went home starved. There was need for mentoring, for discipleship, for training, for trimming, for taming, and for testing and then for showing. As I watched the church, my tears fell that God would take us back to our foundations and help reignite the fire of years ago.

To go to war untrained is the beginning of a colossal loss to the Enemy. To engage in ministry without adequate training and supervision is to shamefully wade into the Enemy's camp and present oneself as prey for slaughter. We must state the obvious: that is, as much as God wants all men to be saved, He is not interested in sending untrained soldiers to the battleground. The search for the souls of the lost is urgent and serious, and this is important and disturbing to the heart of our God, yet He abhors leading men and women unequipped, as a lamb before a wolf. The Lord demands adequate equipping and training before an onslaught, because men jump into ministry when they are about things other than heaven and its purpose and programs. Heaven's and eternity's goal demands adequate and proper training and discipline. The eternal destinies of men and women cannot be handed over to mediocre men who are devoid of spiritual succor or the ordinance to get things done, an example God Himself displays continually.

"And I looked around to see if I could find a man ... and there was none." Because the Lord is of purer eyes than to behold iniquity, He will not smile at wickedness or permit one who has not been weaned to handle the Word of Truth. If He allows this, know that there is an Eli, against whom heaven closed its doors and thus, there is no open vision in the land. In that case, there is an emerging "Ichabod" to be displayed in the church. But that is why we must speak out—to ask you to go back to Bethel and complete training and discipleship work, together with your anointing. That is why God points to the need to discover Him again.

For eons, the prophets and the sons of the prophets (trainees) have attended schools to acquaint themselves of and about ministry work. The Pharisees and Greeks spent years discovering what the mind of God was. There was no shortcut to ministry, no adjunct, what-I-can-get occupation called ministry in our entrepreneurial schemes.

"A disciple is not greater than His teacher, nor a servant greater than his Master but everyone who is perfectly trained will be like his teacher" (Luke 6:40).

Discipleship is about being a disciplined learner. It calls for sacrifice and dedication. It requires obedience and mentoring. It is therefore important that the trainee submits and learns. I see some young folks contending for the pulpit. I see them jumping into ministry with a loud acclaim and a heavy dose of the Spirit. Great! But they must go back to Bethel, to the school of disciples, and engage in studies under a mentor. Read Galatians 1:11–17 about Paul and then: "Then after three years I went up to Jerusalem to see Peter and remained with him for fifteen days" (Galatians 1:18).

Listen to Paul again:

"I knew a man in Christ above fourteen years ago, (whether in the body, I cannot tell; or whether out of the body, I cannot tell: God knoweth;) such a one caught up to the third heaven. ... How that he was caught up into paradise, and heard unspeakable words, which it is not lawful for a man to utter. Of such a one I will glory: yet of myself I will not glory, but in mine infirmities" (2 Corinthians 12:2, 4–5 KJV).

Paul concluded by saying he would come to visions and revelations. That is a good example for me—to keep tabs on learning and being a disciple, never taking a leave of absence or jumping into the battle without adequate training and equipping. I would be dreaming to assure myself that I could take on the Enemy in battle as a street kid and not have a strong backup before attacking. Our backup is Christ Jesus and the strategies with regard to using the tools received in training.

Consider the Catholic Church or the Anglican Church or even the Methodist Church. Have you wondered why their strategy is sustainable— why they form such a force among the people and government? Simple: they trained their ministers and have better strategies. They don't ask a new convert with deep pockets to start a church. Such a person does not even lead prayer in a small group, because he has not been trained. Fourteen years of training in the Roman Catholic Church seminary is not a joke. There is something to learn from that. You need to be trained before you take to the pulpit. An "easy come, easy go" ministry is not God's design for you. You have a lot to share if only you will hide from public life and go back to the training classroom. There, God will infuse some fire in your bones, and then your showing will come. With all thy getting, get trained.

The Power to Perform
The Holy Spirit (Joel 2:25–28)

He was present, self-infused, and an active participant in the wave that cleaned out the confusion and the dark end of the earth in the first chapter of Genesis. He was in a high-level meeting that decided to form and make man, creating his very nature and style in dust, soon named man. When God breathed into man, this guy was the one who came into that man. So across the sphere and inside of you, the Spirit cannot be ignored. He is a personality, the third personality in the trinity and the power of God. He is the Holy Spirit.

First Corinthians 12 points to the gifts (various ways) He manifests in men, and Galatians 5:22–25 explains His character and the attitudes by which those who are filled by Him (the fruit) should live. In John 7:37–39, Jesus calls on all to come and drink from the waters of the Spirit, to be empowered, and to do exploits for the Lord. Anything done outside the influence of the Spirit is carnal, an activity done in the flesh. The result of such activity is usually short-lived and does not receive heaven's approval. It does, however, invite the ovation and clamor of the world.

Paul asked the Ephesian brethren, "Have been baptized in the Holy Spirit since you believed?" (Acts. 19:2). They had not been baptized in the name of the Lord Jesus. This brings us to actionable scenes in this study.

- You must seek (thirst and hunger for) the Holy Spirit's baptism (Isaiah 55:1–5; John 7:37–39).
- You must open up for His infilling (Acts 2).
- You must operate in the anointing (1 Corinthians 12).
- You must not offend or quench the Holy Spirit.
- You must feed Him with the Word of God.

Are you filled with the gifts of the Holy Spirit? Are you baptized in the Holy Ghost? Do you bear the fruit of the Holy Spirit?

Go to a spiritual mentor or pastor to pray for you now!

The power to perform is in/with the Holy Spirit. To enjoy the Christian life, you must walk in the Spirit, pray in the Spirit, sing in the Spirit—do everything in the Spirit. This is where you draw the joy and peace that comes with serving the Lord in the midst of crisis and offense.

"But they that wait upon the Lord shall renew their strength; they shall mount up with wings like eagles, they shall run and not be weary, they shall walk and not faint" (Isaiah 40:31 KJV)

Preparing for Enlargement

If we pour old wine into a new wineskin, the wineskin might burst. This is a mismatch (Matthew 9:14–17). So fresh vigor is necessary for an enlargement. To experience increase and enlargement, we must do the following:

1. Wait on the Lord (Isaiah 40:28–31). This means to go on a retreat and devote time to prayers and studying the Word of God, alone.
2. Be diligent to get Him to talk to and reveal something (call it having a vision). Revival comes when we begin to see (Hosea 2:1–3; 3:1, 2). Jesus withdrew Himself and prayed. When did you last withdraw yourself to seek the face of God? (Mark 1:32–35; 2:3, 13; 3:1–15).
3. Cast away the old man in you. Change your ways. Mr. Flesh seems to dominate every sphere of your life. The works of the flesh are manifest (Galatians 5:19–21). Flesh shows up in ministry as well as in your home, your workplace, and your daily activities. And they that do such things are none of His. Stop the gossip, lies, forgery, fornication, adultery, malice, and envy. Notice that flesh will always dominate the spirit if you allow it. Ask Ishmael and Isaac, or Esau and Israel, or even Cain and Abel. You must kill Mr. Flesh. Mortify therefore your members … (Colossians 3:1–5).

Set Yourselves Apart
Joshua 5:1–9; Habakkuk 1:3; Ezra 3:1–10; 11–13

God is not far from you. He desires an intimate relationship with you. When God wants to do a specific project, He does not work with a crowd. He looks for a man, just an ordinary man. This man must be called, trained, trimmed, and tested. He must be circumcised. Circumcision involves the use of sharp knives (Genesis 17:10–14; Joshua 5:1–9). This means there will be some bleeding, some pain, and a waiting period for healing. Circumcision is a branding label for your inheritance. It reinstates the covenant and ushers in the promise.

Salted Cruse ... Bring Me a Cruse!

You must be familiar with high-sucrose concentrates (HSC), which are used to make foods sweet. God wants us to sweeten our environments and add flavor to the lives around us. It seems to me that God has been searching for vessel—a cruse—to fill and use. He says, "Bring me a new cruse." What happened to the old cruse? It is not good for the big stuff that the Lord is ready to unleash. And this vessel must be one of a kind. No wonder the Lord still seeks a man—just a man. God needs a new cruse—a clean, salted vessel—in which to fill His Spirit.

But sometimes we find an old cruse that offers itself to be filled with salt. It does not receive divine acceptance because it is out of divine course, even if it fasts and prays. Fasting and prayer do not remove the root of evil in a man. They suppress the flesh for a while (and if you are wise, you use the opportunity of fasting and praying to kill Mr. Flesh), but the Spirit of God can war with the dirt and decay in your heart if you allow Him. It is only at the altar, before the blood-stained cross, where the blood of Jesus atones for the lost, that you find cleansing. It does not come cheap. It comes with a heart rending—a tear for sin committed, a prayer that places an order for grace and mercy.

Perfect Fit for Ministry
2 Samuel 11 (The Uriah Example)

In this passage, Uriah is an emptied, yielded, and cleaned-out soldier of the Lord. He is a proselyte. He is detached from the world and has a firm grip on a passion and mission. His eyes are fixed on Jesus and His heavenly glory. Give him a close look, and you'll see he is estranged from filthy lucre, as he has been schooled in the wilderness and has been beaten into shape, never conforming to the world's design and mold. He has an unbending zeal for knowledge and is ready to die for the course of the one who died for him and rose again. He is adorned with the fruit of the Spirit, as we see him give no room to the Evil One and his agents. He is undaunted, resilient, and ready to go on, even in the face of adversity. That is the man God is looking for. God found Uriah the Hittite, a proselyte from another nation. God brought him into the kingdom. Can God find you?

The Winning Strategy: to Occupy until He Comes
Luke 19:12–27

God is looking for a man who will say no to the Devil, who will say, "Enough is enough!" He is looking for a man of prayer (Matthew 11:11–14; 2 Corinthians 10:4–6; Ephesians 6:10–16). We must learn to employ a strategic prayer pattern—a prayer according to God's will. This is a concise prayer against the Devil, the type that touches God's heart. This is prayer of faith.

Those who employ such a strategy stand out with a divine mandate and are not given to popular opinion; they are not "yes men." They mind the things of God, follow after the Spirit's leading, and are determined to complete the work with the Lord. Their passion and gaze are toward heaven and the course of Christ, and thus they engage in intercessory combat. This winning strategy is prayer. It is a talk with the Father that produces a response.

When this happens, you are sure there were discussions and instructions. You know that you have been empowered and commissioned to engage in an assignment—an assignment that changes the world. That's the prayer I am talking about.

It's a Wet Call

I wrote at the beginning of 2013 that I did not qualify for a position on the pulpit, yet my occupation and privileged access into people's lives seemed to stretch endlessly toward the time to quit. Like every ol' buck my age, I found it difficult to understand the many prophecies that dotted headlines, year after year, without reference to the Holy Writ. I wondered if I was becoming a sour ol' goat and how a young guy like me had racked up so many years, oblivious to today's easy run gospel. In retrospect, I should have seen it coming.

A few days into the new year, a friend called just before midnight and asked, "Did I wake you?" Maybe the question was intended to be unapologetic remorse—like, "Hey, Pastor, take the call even though it's late." And so we chatted. We talked about people's operations and argued over New Year's resolutions. I told him about the high fiber in my diet and my resolve to bid soda farewell. He claimed his joints could predict the weather more accurately than the Weather Channel. We talked about adult education stuff and a sentence in the assigned reading list three or four times before the information would sink in. I helped my friend to realize that we are as young as we feel. He was quick to ask me to try out with my teenager on the open soccer field.

With the appearance of the new, the old become stale and seems to repel many. The many prophetic overtures and claims just drown my psyche and send me back to Scriptures about these outbursts that are alien to divine instruction. That is not my problem; I care more about a mandate I got the night before my friend called. I was quick to assure myself that the message was without blemish and that it was from God and in sync with Scriptures. Here's what I was instructed to share with you:

"Go, under My guidance, raise a people given to worship, deep in exhaustive teaching of the Word, rich in compassion, powered by the anointing, laced with contagious love, and living the dominion life exuberantly."

- worship—unhindered worship
- exhaustive teaching of the Word
- compassionate lifestyle
- anointing, even for the anointed
- love that is contagious
- living in dominion

I stood speechless, dazed with some power that strips a man of whatever is macho in his self-esteem. I am not a prophet or the son of a prophet; I'm just a mere man—fragile, limited, unworthy, rotten, and cleaned. Then God—the supreme, almighty Creator, the all-knowing and all-sufficient—spoke. When He sits down, He uses the earth as a footstool, and as He tries to clean sand and dust off His feet, they constitute the clouds of the earth. Just imagine that! The air off His breathe displaces mountains and rips apart the ends of the earth with adjoining hills. He is and will ever be—neither created nor subject to election. That's the one who speaks to a mortal man. I take that seriously. As I age, He is ageless. Do you understand the worthlessness of man, the unworthiness? That is why man must listen and obey God.

The reason for your calling is not necessarily to make men rich by pronouncements, nor is it a scheme to make men comfortable in their usual state of depravity and sin. It is not to forcibly make them think highly of you, especially in the face of dwindling spiritual reach of the soul. Your calling is to fix lives and save the lost—to encourage and teach, to show compassion and love; to demonstrate the Lord as though He were physically present, walking the aisle with you. The purpose is to redo the broken altar that your peers messed up and undo the habitation of the Devil, institutionalizing righteousness and equity in your community (starting with the church, as the pulpit is the hub of activity). That's the purpose. As we go through the ages, may I invite you to stroll down memory lane to check if you are given to frivolities and fantasies in ministry, to a quest to gain and fill your stomach with a scheme to kill and stampede others for a position—a wanton display of kingship over God's elect. Check your heart and return. I call you to the real stuff, the wet-call stuff.

My friend Ron Walters, the senior vice president of Ministry Relations for WRFD radio in Columbus, Ohio wrote to encourage me to stay the course as an old-school person. He wrote, "I celebrate my age; it's made me a wealthy man. Not because of the silver in my hair or the gold in my teeth, but because of the many adventurous miles on my soul's odometer. And I'm determined to keep cruising as long as there's tread on the tires."

As you decide to stroll the path of worship and exhaustive teaching and doing the work, with a complete surrender to compassion under the anointing, you will discover that God will fill your trenches with a full measure of enviable living. It is the Father's desire to give you the kingdom. It starts with an obedient heart and a transformed passion to live for Him. Friend, don't be swayed by the many prophesies. Get back to your God and obtain firsthand prophecy for your life and ministry. You can join us in our wet-call mandate. As you join me, don't forget I'm an old school, rusty fella, with whom you'd enjoy doing the race. Bon voyage! Welcome aboard!

Aging and Living to Your Full Potential
(Provided by Ron Walters, Sr. VP Ministry Relations, Salem Communications)

"Is there anything more natural than aging? You must refuse to give in to the stereotypical old-age phobia. And I'm buoyed by others who feel the same. Consider "old folks" such as:

- Grandma Moses, who at age seventy-six began her iconic career in painting
- Colonel Harland Sanders, who sixty-five perfected those eleven herbs and spices
- Golda Meir, who at seventy-one became prime minister of Israel
- Laura Ingalls Wilder, who at sixty-five cranked out her first novel, *Little House on the Prairie*
- Irene Wells Pennington, who in her nineties took control of the family business and turned a $600 million oil company into some serious money
- Melchora Aquino, who at eighty-four led the Philippines' fight for independence from Spain
- Mahatma Gandhi, who at seventy-eight became the preeminent leader in freeing India from British rule
- Oscar Swahn, who at sixty-four won an Olympic gold medal and eight years later won an Olympic silver medal
- And Caleb, who said, "Here I am today, eighty-five years old! I am just as strong today as the day Moses sent me out; I'm just as vigorous to go to battle as I was then. Now give me this hill country!"

There's plenty of fight left in many of us.

Then there was Abraham. When we first meet the patriarch, the old boy was seventy-five years old and settling into the quiet life of a retirement village in Ur of the Chaldeans. Although he and Sarah had no children, they had even less hope of birthing one while in "the home." But they did have a large extended family and many possessions. They had retired well. Therefore, in this last chapter of their lives, the twilight years, they would recline and reminisce about a full and adventurous life. For Abraham, life had just begun. He was to experience a full stretch of a walk with God and with people in and around Canaan.

Life expectancies had already decreased dramatically by this point (the longevity of Methuselah and Noah was ancient history to Abraham). And whereas Noah did most of his ark building when he was in his five hundreds, Abraham had reached his peak age. This septuagenarian knew his best days had passed. But then, he got a call.

God was on the line, telling Abraham to pack up the family, move all their belongings (lock, stock, and barrel) to an unknown place called Canaan.

Abraham did it—without reason, without promise, without a map, without a GPS, and without question. He said good-bye to his comfy confines to relocate in an unknown world.

Nearly two thousand miles later, this obedient traveler arrived in his new home. Only then did God offer His promise to give Abraham a son and all this new land as an inheritance to his descendants.

For Abraham, the best that life had to offer came in his later years. New promises, a new name, a new family—these were all gifts given to accompany his senior status. No wonder this patriarch is prominently listed in the Bible's Hall of Faith! It wasn't age that gained him entrance. Rather, it was his willingness to believe the impossible and obey the unthinkable, despite his age. "By faith, Abraham, when he was called, obeyed ... and he went out, not knowing where he was going."

Ministry is like a reservoir. The longer you serve, the wider and deeper that reservoir becomes. And the surest way to fill that reservoir is to age. There's something about a long, rich life that can't be acquired without living it. As a very wise man once said, "A gray head is a crown of glory."

This aging story reminds me that the making of a man of God is not a tale told in a moment, not a dream realized in a day. It is not a quick fix.

Men—real men, who trade tackles and engage in combatant operations with and against satanic forces—are made. God makes them.

I feel obliged to point you to where God has set the provisions He has made ready, to prepare you for something bigger than what you think you are. He is about to elicit a great explosion out of you, if you agree.

Where God Makes His Men (Thanks to Brother Gbile Akanni)

For any man to take up God's assignment, that man must be called, equipped, and sent to do specific things. Men who have made their mark on God's program for humanity have been made, if God is to give that man His authority over others and circumstances. There is usually a place where such people are made, and there also is a time (usually a process of time) during which God remolds the man into His choice of shape and form. Christians are therefore expected to undergo these phases. Where does God really make His men?

➤ Made in the Wilderness

Several men of God have had bitter experiences or famine or wilderness experiences in their bid to fulfill God's plans for their lives. The purging and cleanup exercise by God is somehow necessary as a result of or maybe a carry-over from the world, or as a result of the many cucumbers, garlic, and onions such people ate while in Egypt. The Lord needed to purge or clean out their vessels so that He might fully fill them with new glories and power. Some are God-ordained so that His will comes to bear on such lives. Consider these experiences:

- Abraham (Genesis 12:10–12; famine, death of spouse, landed properties seized)
- Isaac (Genesis 26:1–6; famine)
- John the Baptist (Luke 1:80; 3:1–3; sent into wilderness, ate locusts and honey, sent to prison for preaching righteousness and got beheaded in there)

- Moses (Exodus 3:1–3; sent into the wilderness with animals as companions)
- Paul (Acts 9:1–28:31; famine, impoverishment, shipwreck, stoned, beaten)

After the wilderness experience, there is usually an empowerment. Jesus returned in the power of the Holy Ghost.

Question 1 What are the features of famine? (Deuteronomy 1:19; 8:15).

Question 2.What spiritual implications do these experiences confer on a servant of God? (1 Corinthians 4:11; 2 Corinthians 6:4, 5; 11:23; 1 Thessalonians 3:3–4).

Question 3. How does God create deserts or wilderness around the lives of His servants? (Deuteronomy 32:9–12; 8:1–14; Zechariah 13:9; Isaiah 48:10; 1 Peter 1:7; 4:12).

Question 4. What was the motivation for men of old who engaged in their wilderness experiences and did not seek a shortcut out?

Question 5. At what point in a man's life does he leave for public ministry? (Mark 3:2; Galatia 1:11–12; Exodus 3:11–13; 4:1–4).

Evaluate your wilderness experience. Share how you overcame your experience and how it remolded you.

➢ Made in the Presence of God

When the Lord Jesus Christ set out to call His apostles, He had three things in mind: that they might be with Him, that they might preach the gospel, and that they might cast out devils (Mark 3:14–15). In the presence of God, servants of the Lord Jesus Christ are meant to do the work. Today, we are enjoined to go back to Bethel, a place of communion with God, a place where we can hear God speak to our hearts and thus worship Him. We are mandated to dwell in the house of God and receive power. Consider these Scriptures and read the following passages:

> Psalm 15:1–5
> Exodus 19:10–11; 15–17
> Isaiah 1:16–18
> Jeremiah 4:14
> 2 Corinthians 7:1
> 2 Timothy 2:21
> James 4:8
> 1 John 3:3

The invitation into the presence of God is not a one-time or sporadic visit. It is a lifetime thing; a call to live there and be sufficiently drowned in the rivers of living waters and lost in the presence of the Almighty.

From Matthew 25:1–13, what is the state of servants of God who are dry of anointing?

What are the traits of a minister who worships from afar? (Mark 14:54; Exodus 24:9–12; Jeremiah 23:25–30).

What are the likely evidences of a man who dwells in God's presence? (Exodus 24:12; 1 Kings 17:1–5, 8; 2 Timothy 3:16–17; Romans1:16, 28).

There must be a standing in His presence before we can think of a Mount Carmel experience. The glory of His presence reveals itself. It purifies the heart and separates us from the world. It commissions us to serve (Isaiah 6:1–10; Exodus 34; 29–35; Matthew 17:1–3; 2 Peter 1:16–18).

➢ Made in the Place of Prayer

Closely related to the presence of God in the life of a servant of God is the place of prayer. It is an important place in the making of a minister. Consider these Scriptures:

> Luke 3:21, 22
> Acts 9:11, 12, 17–19
> 1 Chronicles 4:9–10
> 2 Chronicles 1:7–12
> Luke 1:13

How does prayer make a man of God? Some personalities get themselves involved in the place of prayer. Find out who these personalities are from Luke 22:40–44; Romans 8:26; and Hebrews 7:25–27.

Real prayers that aim at results and make an impact on men's lives and thus have relevance in God's programs are not piecemeal prayers. They are prayers that affect people and are potent enough to show the power of the Most High. James 5 says it all: Elijah was a man of like passion, meaning he was a man in flesh and blood but travailed before God until he received results. He engaged in prayers of supplication and in intercessory combat with the Enemy. Joshua engaged the Enemy, and he changed the course of the setting of the sun until he gained victory over the Enemy. God can change His plans by reason of your prayers. Some prayers are made with bitter agony of the soul, such that sweat drops are likened to "great drops of blood" (Luke 22:40–44; 2 Corinthians 12:7–12).

Prayer pits two wills against each other: God's will and man's will. Most often, God's will prevails. The servant of God stands as a priest on behalf of the people (Exodus 28:1–25; 1 Peter 2:7–10; Colossians 1:16–28). The purpose of God for your calling is not for any show or shame but for the following reasons:

- to show forth His glory and beauty in a mortal vessel
- to present every man perfect before Christ Jesus at His appearing
- to teach and demonstrate the power of God to principalities and powers of darkness

Thus, it requires us to enter into the Holy of Holies, knowing that lives depend on us to go to heaven, to present them before the Lord (in matters of life and godliness), and to call the attention of heaven on their behalf. As Aaron was charged to bear the names of the twelve tribes on his shoulders as he entered the presence of God, so should we bear the burdens of the church before the Lord. This is the high point of intercessory and supplicating prayers in which we must engage.

➢ Made in the Place of Studying the Word of God

The Lord Jesus declared, search the Scriptures, for in them you think you have life, they are which speak of me (John 5:39). Paul, in his writing, urged Timothy to study, to show himself approved unto God, a workman who needed not be ashamed, rightly dividing the word of truth (2 Timothy 2:15). The need to study cannot be overemphasized. We study to equip ourselves and to gain knowledge of God, of the state of man and society, and of our profession and the economy. We know that knowledge is power. This power is directly linked with our calling. We need to know what we are called to do in the ministry, and this comes from studying. Study these Scriptures:

> 2 Timothy 4:1–5; 11–13
> Colossians 4:17
> Galatians 1:15–18; 4:1–7
> 2 Corinthians 12:1–7

Faith comes by hearing (listening to or reading and studying) the Word of God. Faith is shaped and empowered by knowledge and doctrine. These are subsequently rooted in what you are able to dig out of the Scriptures. The parchments are still needed in today's ministry, and you need to be equipped with the right tools and knowledge before you dive into ministry. Come—let's study together. I desire to make a disciple out of you.

CHAPTER 2

Get It Right the First Time

"You do not get a second chance to make a first impression"

Born Again? Meaning and Experience

To repent and be converted is to change from an old style of living or doing things—to decide to stop moving in that direction and turn around, and start moving in the opposite path, to start a new way of life. It is to shift from an old paradigm to a new course.

When the Devil went to Eve in the garden of Eden and convinced her that she would be like God if she ate the forbidden fruit, both Adam and Eve sold their position with God and their rights as custodians and superintendents on earth, as carriers of divine nature (an embodiment of the godhead: Father, Son, Holy Spirit), to the Enemy.

Sin entered into man and the world by that singular act. Man became subject to the whims of the Devil. The whole earth and man himself have been held in bondage and subjected to annihilation and decay, always trembling at the slightest noise from the Devil (Psalm 82:5; Romans 8:19). That was Satan's plan until God, revealed in Jesus, paid the price to buy man back. In a sense, man was kidnapped, and a ransom was required. God paid for a repurchase. That price was the life of His Son, Jesus Christ. This was at the cross of Calvary. With the deal completed, God demands that any man who accepts this offer and believes that Jesus is the Son of

God, confessing his or her sins, will be saved. This is a gateway to eternal life. At this point of change (accept your inadequacy and helpless situation; believe in Jesus Christ to save you from the mire of sin and destruction; confess with your mouth that He is Lord and Savor), the full significance of a new nature or repentance comes to play in your life. It is a decision to lead another life and a movement toward a completely new direction in Christ Jesus.

This is as if you are saying, "Yes, Jesus, you are now completely in charge of my life." The Holy Spirit helps you to enter into this life-changing decision, and this is meant by "born again." So relating repentance to God's original desire for humanity is an occasion whereby man "buys in" to the transaction offered by God, to accept His finished work as a first step. Nobody can lay claim to being born again without the step of genuine repentance.

"And Jesus answered, most assuredly I say to you, unless one is born again, he cannot see the kingdom of God ... most assuredly I say to you, unless one is born of water and Spirit, he cannot enter into the kingdom of God. That which is born of the flesh is flesh, and that which is born of the Spirit is spirit. Do not marvel that I said to you, 'You must be born again" (John 3:3, 5–7).

The age we live in has modeled certain lifestyles and patterns of behavior to fit into the social, economic, and political design and programs. The result is that the strong man (Satan) is gradually inching in and gaining a firm grip on the souls of men. This satanic model of the world has been released toward the church and, unfortunately, the church or the kingdom's recipients have embraced it and dance and sing along with it. To be born again means more than a "repeat after me" from a pastor. It is more than joining the choir or entreating a congregation with a show of what money can buy, including the cathedrals and estates. It is to have the Spirit of God live inside you on a daily basis, guiding and instructing you on all holy and righteous living. It is a shift from living filthy to living clean before God and man. *It is a conscious and deliberate choice to say no to sin.* It is to have God plant the seed of righteousness in you, perpetually. On a daily basis, you are allergic to sin.

What, then, shall we say? Must we continue in sin so that grace will flourish? Must I use the gospel of love to pretend that I do not see the filth in the church, especially among the pastors and clergy? No, I do not think so! The world and its satanic insurgence into the lifeline of the church is succeeding because we have let it in. We crave the fashions of the world, and we do the things they do in offices and business places, and we hold same political opinions and voting options for the very things that the Word of God classifies as sin.

What, then, would you say when a pastor advises a young woman to go on a seven-day fast, and on the seventh day, she goes to the river, strips herself naked at midnight, gets into the river, and then emerges from it to call on God, seeking a husband? That pastor is not born again. Truly, if there is any sign in his ministry, it is most likely given by the evil spirit from the waters. Do you see why the world is inching into the church? Why power is lacking? Sin shall not have dominion over you, says the Lord. You must repent and be converted.

You may have heard that the moment you give your life to Jesus, everything turns great and wonderful for you, that you'll become a millionaire and all sicknesses and disease will be gone. I wish our flight to heaven took an immediate turn when we are saved, but to repent and be converted means to change your mind and make a choice in your actions. The Lord promises a good life in the kingdom and a refreshing moment in His presence. He will not withhold from you and your family anything good and glorious, because "while the earth remains, seedtime and harvest, cold and heat, winter and summer, and day and night shall not cease" (Genesis 8:22). This passage was after the cleansing and after the overhaul of the filthy earth and evacuation of sinful men in it. God has a pattern of doing things to clean out and refill, to purge and use, and to sanctify and set apart for His glory.

God's intention is to rebrand man and make a son out of the wayward, and in so doing, position him in his original estate, as found in Eden. His plan is to remake man and boast about him before the fallen angels and Satan, to make possible and bestow on man the rights and privileges (the power, the glory, the anointing, and the best any father give to his son) to man. Before this is done, there must be a heart transplant—an exchange of the fallen nature and sinful or corrupted seed that the devil planted at Eden with the Holy Spirit of God. He plans to change your DNA and begin a blood transfusion that will energize and tone up the God nature in you. You need the divine nature again. And that is why I tell you one more time: *you must be born again!*

May the Lord help you as you make this decision, even if you have been a pastor or a bishop or a regular participant in religious activities. It does not matter. Your spirit must be set right. You cannot fight your Maker.

Pray!

1. What does repentance mean? (Hebrews 6:1–2; Acts 3:19; 1 Thessalonians 1:5–10).

It is a firm conscious and personal decision to change from sin (obedience to the Devil) to righteousness in obedience to God. It is not an emotion. (Although your emotions can help move you closer to the cross; do not stop at that point.) Repentance must involve the following:

- Acknowledge that you were born a sinner and you have been sinning (Romans 3:23; John 8:44).
- Believe that Jesus Christ died in your place and is the only One who can help you out of your problems (Acts 4:12).
- Confess your sins (1 John 1:9).
- Ask God for forgiveness and His mercy (Isaiah 55:7).
- Ask for divine ability to forsake your sins (Proverbs 28:13).

2. How important is repentance to us as believers? Were we ever enslaved by any power? (Luke 3:7–9; Galatians 5:22–23).

Genuine repentance is followed by desirable and tangible fruit of the Spirit, like love, peace, patience, and faith. Identify the more evidences from the following passages: Matthew 4:17; Luke 3:1–5; 15:7; Luke 3:14.

Jesus, our Lord and Master, commanded us to repent and be saved. Saved from what? (Act.2:37–38; Acts 17:30–31; 20:20–21).

The disciples preached it and thus we must follow the apostles' doctrine. How? (Matthew 3:1–2)

John the Baptist also preached salvation, being a bridge between the prophets and the dispensation of grace. No one can say he is born again without genuine repentance.

3. What are the dead works from which we have to repent? How can a man's work be regarded as dead?

Sin, the works of the flesh, idolatry, empty religion, and all unrighteousness are the dead works of which we should repent (Hebrews 6:1; Romans 6:21; 1 Corinthians 6:9–11; Galatians 5:19–21; 1 Thessalonians 1:9; Philippians 3:1–3; 2 Timothy 3:8–9 ; Ezekiel 14:6; Ephesians 4:25–31).

4. Elements of Genuine Repentance
   • Conviction: Before any sinner can repent, he must be convicted that he has an urgent need to make his way right with God (Psalms 38:4; 51:3; Acts 2:37).
   • Godly sorrow: This comes because of conviction by the Holy Spirit. It produces repentance (2 Corinthians 7:10).
   Renunciation: True repentance involves grief and hatred for sin, forsaking and turning from it to God. One must renounce sin and express separation from such entanglements with sin, satanic insurgence, and the world system with the mouth and be separated from them in the heart (Isaiah 55:7; Joel 2:13).

5. Distinguish between genuine repentance and remorse.

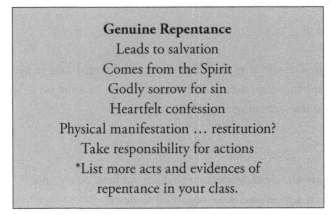

Genuine Repentance
Leads to salvation
Comes from the Spirit
Godly sorrow for sin
Heartfelt confession
Physical manifestation ... restitution?
Take responsibility for actions
*List more acts and evidences of
repentance in your class.

You can be sorry for a wrong-doing, but that does not mean you do not have an intention to do it again. This is remorse—to feel guilty and make a passing motion of saying you are sorry. Repentance is more than that (Psalm 51:1–9, Romans 6:23; 12:1–2; Matthew 27:3–4; Acts 1:25).

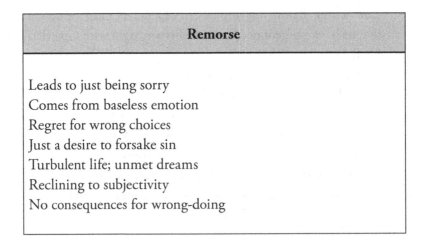

Remorse

Leads to just being sorry
Comes from baseless emotion
Regret for wrong choices
Just a desire to forsake sin
Turbulent life; unmet dreams
Reclining to subjectivity
No consequences for wrong-doing

Genuine repentance is a twofold act: (1) turning away from sin; and (2) turning to God for forgiveness. Turning from sin without turning to God is reformation without regeneration. It is a wishy-washy euphoria that vaporizes with the introduction of heat or pressure from the world. For example, your New Year's resolution that is based on self-will without the help of the Holy Spirit is done with a mind-set of abstaining from or engaging in certain behaviors. Those things can be effectual only when the power to overcome rests on a man. In genuine repentance, we therefore ask God to help us uphold the ethos and worth of godly behavior. He provides the power to do so through His Spirit. This is, in part, why we are baptized in the Spirit.

6. Why is repentance necessary? A friend asks you this question when you urge him or her to surrender his or her life to Jesus, knowing that he or she has led a very good life. How would you answer this question?

Read Isaiah 64:6–7 and Ephesians 2:8–10.

7. There are consequences for our actions and inactions. Consequences; because we have been provided with a choice to do the right thing and instead, we are unbending while doing the wrong thing. Reiterate the consequences with these passages

> A person who fails to repent will perish (Luke 13:5).
> An unreported sin is an unforgiven sin.
> An unforgiven sin will destroy (Psalm 38:3b).

8. What are the results of genuine repentance?

> Romans 5: l, 8; 2 Corinthians 5:16–17; Isaiah 30:15; Acts 3:l9; Psalm 51:7–10, 12–14; Galatians 5:22–23; Luke 15:7–10

Repentance reinstates our positioning in God. It reestablishes our relationship and rights as sons, granting us access to the power that was originally given at Eden. It assures us of the presence of the Godhead and provides cleansing by the blood of Jesus (by faith), assurance of forgiveness, ability to have a fruitful fellowship with God in prayer, peace with God and man, and justification as if sins never occurred within our ranks. It provides joy of salvation and constantly fortifies the hedge around us.

Conclusion

Remember, God is not mocked (Galatians 6:7). Sin will always pay its full price if not repented (Romans 6:23a) and will result in serious consequences if true conversion is not heeded. God is ready to forgive your sins. He is rich in mercy (Psalm 86:5), especially where He finds genuine (heart-searching) repentance. It's worth the effort to call on Him while you can. You will have wonderful times of refreshing from the presence of the Lord.

Memory Verse

"He that covers his sins shall not prosper: but whoever
that confesses and forsakes them shall have mercy"
(Proverbs 28:13).

Notes

CHAPTER 3

Understand What Christ Did for You

Genesis 2:15–20; 3:1–18

When God said, "Let us make man in our image ...and in the likeness of God He made man," I think He simply poured out Himself into man. He imputed the God-nature in man and established him in the right place to operate as "god." No wonder He said, "You are gods and all of you are children of the Most High" (Psalm 82: 6).

Adam was the head of the human race. He represented God on earth in the beginning. He had the right to name all things created by God, and he got God's approval. He controlled and had authority over all creatures. In other words, Adam had *dominion* over everything created, including the lions and all dangerous and wild animals on earth. Adam was living in dominion because he had the God-nature. He shared the kingdom with God. God would come in the cool of the evening to have fellowship with Adam and Eve. What a relationship; what a fellowship with the Father! What does it mean to live in dominion and be part of the kingdom?

The divine nature was in Adam and Eve. This is the nature and DNA of God the Father, God the Son and God the Holy Ghost. Their intricate and intrinsic natures were infused into Adam—their characters and lifestyles; their powers and authorities; their ways and methods of operations; their offices and whatever is called God found their way into

Adam by impartation and empowerment. The divine nature was complete, not less of anything but full of everything in God … in Adam.

Paradise was an excellent place to be. The garden was the epitome of the serenity God planned for human race, an embodiment of peace and a place God enjoyed visiting for fellowship with man. Everything was provided for and all things served for the benefit of man. There, we find Adam dwelling perfectly in peace with his wife, Eve, until something happened.

Adam changed the course of the human race by falling into sin (Romans 5:12). Satan made Adam to believe the following about God:

- That God was a liar (Genesis 2:17; 3:4)
- That God was deceitful and did not have the love of His creatures at heart (Genesis 3:5)
- That God did not want them to live beyond their current state or to their potential
- That God was unfair by not giving them that which was their ultimate good (Genesis 3:5)

Satan denied the very essence of God's character of truth and righteousness and blasphemed God. He spoke irreverently about God and painted God in a bad light.

We discover here that Satan was the accuser and the judge. When men accuse their fellows, stage a trial by proxy, and judge based on what the coalition says, and then there is a problem. There is a replay of a satanic pattern of justice. For Adam, it was a case of a foolish display of leadership positioning (of not going back to God to affirm the allegations) and more, not being there with his wife (who was actually deceived) and not taking responsibility for their actions. Had he cried in repentance and not got into the blame game, God would have listened with pity and forgiveness.

Consequences of the Fall

- Loss of communion and fellowship with God (Isaiah 59:2; Ephesians 2:11–12)
- Spiritual death (Romans 6:23)

- Physical death (Hebrews 9:27)
- Received the nature of sin and debt to sin (Genesis 1:27; 5:3)
- Transferred our fatherhood to the Devil (John 8:44)
- Slave to Satan (Colossians 1:13; 2 Timothy 2:26)
- Loss of God-given authority to the Devil (James 14:30; Luke 4:5–6; Ephesians 6:10–18)
- Loss of dominion over all the works of God (Genesis 1:28)
- Loss of freedom from diseases, sorrow, hardship, and suffering (Genesis 3:16–19)

Devotional

Imagine you were made to function like the angels, to worship and praise God every hour of every day, to run errands and minister to folks below your status and power. You were created to serve. You were created to appear before Him whose eyes ooze with radiant shine that demeans the rays of the sun at its peak; to worship, remain spotless, and orchestrate order and equity on earth. Will you maintain your status, living in your mortal flesh? Do you think man can measure up with the demands of heaven? Will he be able to stand before this God? I do not think so, but grace has provided a platform to stand and relate with the heavenly personalities, to stand before God. What a privilege!

Mercy and Pardon for Sin
Some attributes of God's righteousness

In Him is light, and there is no unrighteousness in Him whatsoever. He is an embodiment of light and truth and life. There is a scepter of righteousness and a standard with which God is typified—a standard and status of behavior devoid of error or omission. He is righteous, and in Him there is no unrighteousness at all. His ways are perfect and true (Psalm 119:137; Jeremiah 23:6; Deuteronomy 32:4; James 45:21).

Love (John 3:16; Romans 5:8), truth (2 Samuel 7:28), eternal life (Exodus 15:18; Revelation 1:8)

God's Mercies ... Try a Shot at Mercy

Describe or tell a story that typifies God's grace and mercy in your life. Mercy is an act of benevolence shown to one who does not deserve it, though guilty of an offense, and in his place, one who is the judge comes to bear the consequences of the offense and declares that the guilty is free, without charge or indebtedness.

In 1992, one of the rich folks in Lagos, Nigeria, gave me about $150,000 cash to start a produce business. This man did not know me and had no ties with my family, nor was he from my relative, but a friend had whispered my name to him as a good and trusted friend with whom he could do business. He invited me over, and we talked about commodities and the produce business. He liked me and gave me the money. I made my first trip for supplies. On my second trip to pay cash to my suppliers (farmers who would not accept checks or money orders), I was attacked by armed robbers who took the money. My world was closed, so to speak. I was unable to eat or drink for about ten days, as I was in great pain and filled with regret for losing what was not mine. I took the police report to my friend and had prepared my house and mind (after much prayer) to turn myself in. I knew the only option left with him was to send me to jail, with or without trial (remember this happened in Nigeria. Processes in Africa are done differently).

I decided to offer myself up before this friend in his Broad Street office. He had not seen me since the robbery occurred. As he gazed through his fine eyeglasses, something told me that the worst was about to happen. My friend and his family were in the top class of society. At their call, police show up to do as commanded; when they sneeze, the Nigeria stock market is readily sick of something. They are filled with an air of importance and have the wherewithal to cause ripples. As I opened the door to his office, there was silence. He took a long, straight look at me, pulled at his glasses, and said, "You mean you want to die because you lost my money? I trusted you well enough to give you the money. I still trust you. Emmanuel, please go take a shower and have some food. Go home and get some rest. You look horrible." That was an act of mercy from a man, mercy for Emmanuel Elendu.

To meet God's holy character of justice (for sin) and love (for the sinful man), the last Adam (Jesus Christ) was sent to break down the barrier between God and man and thus pay the price for the penalty of sin, bringing man back to God. This is mercy from God (Romans 5:17–19; 1 Corinthians 15:21–22, 45–47).

What, Then, Is the New Birth?

It is a spiritual experience that transforms us from the kingdom of darkness into God's kingdom. It is receiving God's life and God's righteousness into our lives. It is both a spiritual and moral change. Christ lives in you by the Holy Spirit. It is not a physical birth; our spirit, not our flesh, is born again. It is so vital an experience that no one can enter into God's kingdom without it (John 3:1–7; 1:12–13; 1 Peter 1:23; Colossians 1:12–13; Ephesians 2:8–10). It is mercy revealed and sent by God to mortal man in exchange for the sins man has committed over the period of ignorance. The new birth is the planting of the seed of God in the heart of man and a regeneration of the heart of man, courtesy of the cleansing power in the blood of Jesus Christ.

The ABC's of the New Birth

Acknowledge that you are a sinner (Romans 3:23; Luke 18:13; Psalm 51:5).

Believe in your heart that Jesus can save you from your sins and sincerely repent of your sins (Acts 3:19; Luke 13:3).

Confess your sins to God (1 John 1:19).

Forsake or turn away from your old sinful ways (Isaiah 55:7; Proverbs 28:13).

Believe in Him and in the sacrifice He made for you (John 3:16; 2 Corinthians 5:21).

Receive Him into your heart by faith and thereafter thank God for saving you (John 1:11–12; Ephesians 2:8).

There is a tendency to play the blame game—to blame someone else, including God, for our predicament in sin or even the situation in which we find ourselves. That is natural with man. We do not want to take responsibility for our actions or inactions that result to negative outcomes. For example, Adam responded defensively when God confronted him with his sin at Eden. He blamed Eve, Eve blamed the serpent, and there the blame game started. Whatever the blame, sin is like a cancer, eating away the fabrics of our souls. In sin we were conceived, and the heart of man is desperately wicked and deceitful, beyond what we know or can imagine. The stain is indelible, almost without remedy, but the blood of Jesus is able to wipe off this stain. It takes a blood solution (of Jesus Christ) to deal with a sin-stained blood of our lives. Do yourself good; try a blood transfusion now.

Just as you can associate a dog with bones, so you can associate every man born of a woman with sins. One thing is certain: any life committed to Jesus Christ cannot be wasted. What are you doing with Jesus Christ?

Memory Verse

> "Therefore if any man be in Christ, he is a new creature:
> old things are passed away; behold all things are become
> new" (2 Corinthians 5:17).

Understanding the New Birth

The creation of man was a joint act, a collaborative effort of God the Father, God the Son, and God the Holy Ghost (Genesis 1:26). It was about setting in place a replication of what was obtainable in the heavens in order for man to be in charge of the earth. God was giving man the authority and dominion to rule the earth. God intended that Adam was to be a complete replication and representation of God on earth. Man was in charge of all things because he had the nature of God, for God gave Adam his very gem of existence, the spirit of God. Man had the fullness of the Godhead dwelling in him. By fullness, I mean an assemblage of the operative and ruling authority of the Godhead (Father, Son, and Holy Ghost). Remember, in the image of the Godhead, Adam was made. So Adam was not deficient in any way. He was not supposed to be diminished or intimidated by circumstances or by any form of subtitle by the Devil. He was in full possession of power and authority from the God head.

"And God blessed them and God said unto them, Be fruitful and multiply and replenish the earth and subdue it and have dominion over the fish of the sea, and over the fowl of the air and over every living thing that moveth upon the earth" (Genesis 1:28–31).

This was God's plan for man. But man fell to the lie of the Devil—"Eat of this fruit and you will be like God." Adam did not have to experiment on this. for he was already a "god" in charge of the earth. He was not to take instructions from the Enemy because God was, to Adam, a colleague and a mentor. There was enough spiritual romance and fellowship with God and enough work to occupy any man; there was enough grace and companionship. But Adam chose to listen to the Enemy through his wife. Alas, every authority, power, and dominion was taken away. Man became like a piece of bread to the very things that he had control over. He became dehumanized, without power and authority, and without the vigor of life, as the source of life was withdrawn, and the fountain became bitter.

But in God's recovery plan, He sent his Son to redeem man, to restore the positioning of man in the Godhead in bodily form. For in Jesus, all things consist (Colossians 2:6–12).

Why is the new birth so important?

The natural man is spiritually dead and therefore cannot obey or understand or please God (Romans 8:6–8; Jeremiah17:9; Ephesians 2:3).

The new birth gives eternal life. It repositions man and grants him access to the Godhead. He is able to access God and have fellowship with his Creator again (John 3:16).

The natural man is corrupt in his affections and perverse in his will (Galatians 5:19–21; Mark7:21–23). The new birth affects our tastes, habits, desires, choices, passions, and pursuits in life.

The natural man is on a naturally sloppy course to destruction (Proverbs 14:12; 12:15).

The new birth guarantees that our names are written in God's Book of Life (James 3:3–5; Revelation 20:15).

What did Jesus do for you as a natural man? Explain with personal experiences, please.

- Saved us from sin (Matthew 1–21; John 1:29; Matthew 26:28; 1 John 3:5)
- Delivered us from the works and power of the Devil (Colossians 1:13; 1 John 3:8)
- Paid the penalty for sin and removed the course of God upon man (Galatians 3:13; 2 Corinthians 5:21)
- Reconciled man (the offender) to God (the offended) by acting as a mediator between God and man (2 Corinthians 5:17–21; 1 Timothy 2:5)
- Opened the way to God (Matthew 27:50–53; John 14:6; Luke 1:79).
- Registered our names in God's Book of Life (Luke 10:20; Revelation 20:15)

Hindrances to Salvation

Satan has blinded the eyes of many people, such that despite several obstacles God allows to be created on their paths to hell, they are adamant and have hardened their hearts to the light of the gospel of Jesus Christ. In other words, the only vestige of genuine repentance associated with their Savior, Jesus Christ, was the day they responded to the altar call (2 Corinthians 4:4). Sad to say that these folks have been lured away from the faith for reasons we may uncover in the following passages.

The following could hinder a man from receiving the salvation made available by God through Jesus Christ: 2 Corinthians 5:11; 1 Peter 4:18; 2 Timothy 2:19.

Can you identify the one(s) the Devil can easily use against you?

- Fear of persecution (2 Timothy 3:12; John 17:14–16; 1 Peter 2:19–23)
- Comfort and riches (1 Timothy 6:9–10; Proverbs 10:17–22; Luke 16:13)
- Much intellectual or human achievement (1 Timothy 6:20–21; 1 Corinthians 2:5; Philippians 3:3–10)

- False security (Isaiah 31:1; Psalm 97:7)
- Self-righteousness (Isaiah 64:6; Romans 10:3)
- Worldliness (James 4:4; 2 Timothy 4:10; 1 John2:16)
- Lust for position or power (Ecclesiastics 2:9–11; Psalm 62:11)
- Covetousness (Luke 12:15; Proverbs 15:16)
- Desire to please man (1 Samuel 31:4; 2 Samuel 1:5–16)
- Religious activities (Matthew 5:20)
- Some definite life ambitions (Ecclesiastics 9:12)
- Besetting sins (Hebrews 12:1)
- Ignorance (1 Timothy 1:13)

Evidences of the New Birth

Discuss noticeable evidences of the new birth in your life since you openly confessed Jesus Christ as your Lord and Savior.

- A changed life (2 Corinthians 5:17; Colossians 3:1–3)
- A righteous and holy life (1 John. 2: 29; 1 Peter 1:14–16)
- Godly love and love for the Scriptures (1 John 4:7; Acts 7:11)
- Godly fear and obedience to God (Ecclesiastics 12:13)
- An overcoming life (1 John 5:4)
- Witness of the Spirit (Romans 8:16)
- Communion and fellowship with God (1 John 1:3)
- Power to live the Christian life (John 1:12)

How Can We Live This New Life Successfully?
Grace, Mercy, and Truth! Holy Ghost Power and the Anointing

Again, to live by the law is to demean grace and all the finished work of Christ on the cross. The power to live in the dominion and authority that God gave to man at the beginning of creation must come back from the One who withdrew His power and authority. This rechanneling and empowering is of God and Holy Spirit. To struggle and administer man-made laws to do things contrary to the purpose of the coming of Jesus to earth; it runs contrary to defined process and procedure for living in dominion. That would suggest an addition to grace and mercy provided for the fallen man. Thank God for the complete work of grace, the inexhaustible love and passion, and the crescendo in one acclaim at the resurrection power. It is complete, and man only needs to access these resources.

The taste for sin is greatly diminished and fades into oblivion at the face of the power of the Spirit. If the power that raised Jesus up dwells in you it is made active and gets into action. Then sin will, undoubtedly, lose its taste and power in you. There is a God-nature that swells from inside your bowels and fills you up at conversion. The fullness of the Godhead resides in you. This is our major resource reservoir. When we live in the consciousness of this and take our positions in the kingdom of God, that mind-set directs our thinking, behavior, purposes, plans, intents and actions. Then sin will be far from us. According to Scriptures, "sin will not have dominion over you." When we live and move with the mind-set of the presence of God, of Christ dwelling and walking with us daily as we talk to Him and communicate with Him as a friend, then it's easy to live the kingdom lifestyle. For sin shall not have dominion over you, but you will reign in dominion over sin and the world system (1 John.5:4). Though Christ came to fulfill the law, the law on its own did not bring a tangible result in reconciling man to God; Jesus Christ did. To live the free course of divine nature should not be a struggle, because the power of the Holy Spirit inside of you makes necessary the free flow. But we have a mandate to make the power active and to sustain the power and increase its flow. Below are some of the many ways to keep the fire glowing:

Study the Word of God: 1 Peter 2:2l; Psalm 119:103; 2 Timothy 2:15.

How do you develop a regular and consistent study life of the Word?

Mention the different types of study in which you may engage.

Always praying (1 Thessalonians 5:17)

With life in the fast lane and the quest for satisfying daily needs, there must be a place for a deep search of what God is saying and wants us to do. In the face of these, how do we pray to gain direction and obtain instruction as we go?

There are ways to pray, and there are ways not to pray. State these very succinctly.

Ways to pray:

Ways not to pray:

Continuous fellowship with the brethren (Hebrews10:25; Psalm 27; Acts 4:32–37).

The advent of Internet has driven the church to obtain its nourishment from a drive-through joint, a makeshift device that churns half-baked Christians and ill-prepared preachers to the pulpit without a foundation and a counsel. Fellowship remains a lifeline to Christians, especially when they dwell together, one-on-one.

Where do you worship on Sundays and Wednesdays?

Total submission and obedience to the Christ (James 4:7; John 14:15; 5:14)

Witnessing Christ to others (Mark 16:15; Matthew 5:14–15)

How do you share your faith?

With personal testimony (your conversion story)?
With current events happening in society?
With your success?

With your situation?

With world uncertainties?

Summary

Considering what we have learned, a born-again Christian *must* be different from those who are not. This difference should be evident in words, thoughts, and actions (who you are and what you put on, hear, see, or touch) of the believer. Also, a born-again Christian must let go of old patterns of life (sinful) and do away with every form of questionable, unwholesome relationships. Have you had this experience? Change comes from within and then shows to the outer world. Change ought to take place.

Memory Verse

> "Neither is there salvation in any other: for there is none
> other name under heaven given among men, whereby
> we must-be saved" (Acts 4:12).

Certificate of New Birth

I, submit/surrender my life to Christ Jesus as my Lord and Savior. I accept His sacrificial death on the cross as the only remedy to my sins. From this day forward, I will serve, obey, and live for Him, by God's grace.

Date

Witnesses

Reflections

Nicodemus must have been one of the finest and smartest in his class. He trained in Greek and Hebrew as well as in the Aristocratic curriculum for a doctorate in divinity and theology. He led the Jews in their quest to discover the true and only one God. In studying the deity and religions surrounding other gods of the people of the hill countries, Nicodemus delivered polished, intelligent discourses on subjects of religious interest. Nicodemus reminds me of my general studies professor at the University of Nigeria in 1982, who was a Marxist proponent. He ridiculed Jesus in our general studies class. Because he knew me closely, he always would ask me if Jesus attended a college or had a degree or portfolio behind His worth. Of course, my Lord was a Jewish carpenter, unlearned and unscripted. He taught those who supervised Nicodemus.

As a youth, I threw back the dart to my professor but to no avail. One day, I drove to his house to ask if I could talk with him on matters of religion, depravity, sinful life, and life after death. It was a long discussion. The result was that under deep remorse, he accepted that the life he led was not the right one but said that it was too late to go back, because he already was in the Marxist movement. He acknowledged the void and confessed he had put his girlfriend in the family way, the result of which was that he had been mandated to marry her, contrary to his wishes. It was a sober moment, but my professor refused to repent of his sins or yield to Jesus Christ as Savior and Lord. Somehow, there was a void in his heart, and that void that could not be filled with semantics or religious terminology. Nicodemus sought reality and the essence of living; he sought for the true meaning in life but could not find any solution to the many questions that trailed him. For some time, he tried to fill his void with an alcoholic pacifier or some form of the "ego of the man," but it wouldn't just go. Faced with the reality that someday he would stand before God to account for his life, Nicodemus made up his mind to seek help. He secretly went to Jesus by night. "Hey, guy, what must I do to be accepted by God and be a part of His kingdom?" he asked.

One can become a member of a family by birth or adoption. The new birth is the regeneration of the natural man in such a way that one is given a new heart and a new spirit to lead into a new sense of choices and preferences in life. This is guided by a divine power that propels him or her into a new lifestyle, a new and positive way of thinking, always prompted to do right, to the glory of Him who gave the new power and nature (John 1:12–13; Galatians 4:5; Ephesians 5:30–32; 1 Corinthians 5:16–17).

Here's another testimony from my early years in college:

"And that He died for all; that they which live should not henceforth live unto themselves, but unto him which died for them and rose again" (2 Corinthians 5:15).

Living the Resurrected Life!
Restored, Transformed, Empowered

Cool, breezy, and quiet, close to the ancient gates toward the agriculture farm stood Akpabio Hall, University of Nigeria, where student union presidents lived, along with a few of us who supported them. As elevated as the hall was, the nobility-cum-elegance welcomed every visitor, especially when the lights were turned on. This fateful night, however, there was nothing noble or welcoming to our room. Chaos and unruly cries for help filled the air. Mr. Onye ran into room 425, sweating profusely, his eyes bulging. He cried, "Pray before I die, I say. Pray for me! Please pray for me. That bird will soon stop singing, and I will be a dead man. Pray for me."

Daniel Mbiwan and I tried to understand the situation. The situation demanded a prayer of supplication and intercession. Onye was led to Christ in the wee hours of Monday, and as we concluded with an amen, immediately the bird forcibly flew away with a noisy, wild wind. It sang as it flew.

Onye was an occultist who had been asked to pay the ultimate price that night—the price of death—but Jesus set him free. The resurrected life is one of restoration, transformation, and power. Onye had an encounter that transformed his life, and going forward, Jesus led his life. Romans 8:11 says that the Spirit that raised up Jesus dwells in us.

"You must be kidding," I hear you say. God means what He says: to restore you to your original dignity. To restore means to reinstate, bring back, reestablish, return. It brings back to life that which was dead. "Wherefore, as by one man sin entered into the world, and death by sin; and so death passed upon all men, for that all have sinned" (Romans 5:12). As I read through Scriptures from the Bible, I lifted this one, which is worthy of sharing:

"Know ye not that the unrighteous shall not inherit the kingdom of God? Be not deceived: neither fornicators, nor idolaters, nor adulterers, nor effeminate, nor abusers of themselves with people, nor thieves, nor covetous, nor drunkards, nor revilers, nor extortionist, shall inherit the kingdom of God. And such were some of you: but ye are washed, but ye are sanctified, but ye are justified in the name of the Lord Jesus, and by the Spirit of our God" (1 Corinthians 6:9–11).

The experience of the new birth is worth owning ... and that is why we dance and spin.

SPINNING, DANCING, EVOLVING

He gazed with a frenzied motion into the dancing congregation, wondering what got them into chants of victory and spurious joy. They danced as though the mayhem of economic and social news was not for them. The more the music played, the more their steps got wild—the dance, the joy. It is the reason that He died for them and rose again.

Easter brings a pinch of sad and sweet tastes. Sad, when one thinks of the injustice, the unfair trial, and the crucifixion of One who holds all power and authority, yet this Holy One submitted Himself to mere man to be killed. Sweet, when one thinks of the gain, the full payment (in cash) that Jesus paid on our behalf with His blood for the sins He knew nothing about or how they were orchestrated. In the world of business, we might say that He made an investment with His life (blood) with a future value that is expected to yield great dividends. This future value is a function of the worth of the present value, the time to maturity, the return on investment or the risk associated with this investment.

What is your future value, given the investment Jesus made in your life? No wonder the Scriptures attest, "Eyes have not seen, nor ears heard, nor has it been echoed into the imagination of man the very things God has reserved to them that are His own." (1 Corinthians 2:9) It was this unrevealed glory that energized Jesus for the long haul. When He saw the glory waiting for Him, He endured the cross, agonized under the weight of my sins, and bore the shame and received the scourges and the lashes. It was foresight on His part that encouraged and energized his Spirit. When He saw a flirt, a drunkard, and a shameless, worthless fella like me designed for hell, for a horrifying death, He sought me, made a risky venture; and started the cleanup program.

This is the meaning of Easter for me—that I was once lost, headed toward destruction, and suddenly I found myself decorated with glory and honor and power, to even deal some ballistic blows on him who once ruled my life. Now you understand why I spin and dance and indeed shine in a way that dazzles many. At Calvary, my sins were washed away. Jesus rejuvenated my soul and jazzed life into my frames. That is the reason we dance. We rejoice always. It is because our names have been written in the Book of Life. We are empowered to deal with principalities and powers, wickedness, and all disobedience on earth. Hallelujah—He arose. Amen.

CHAPTER 4

The Mess the Devil Got Us Into ... and How God Cleaned Us Up

Saul was a native of Tarsus, a citizen of Rome, and of the extraction of the Benjamin stock, a Hebrew of the first order and an ardent, unbending religious fanatic who spent fourteen years after his call to the bar under Aristotle, Gamaliel, and the Puritan school of divinity. He was mentored by the zealous Pharisees clique. Saul later went wild against the young church. His intent was to exterminate what seemed to oppose the religious order and of course be decorated with a zealot's garb of "the crusader with a no-nonsense accommodation of new entrants into the order."

Henry Ford had foresight of the need for mini-trucks in the United States, and his F150 sold complete. He was the first entrant into that model of truck. When other competitors (GM, Toyota, and later, Honda) tried to copy him, he was already on top with a market share of over 70 percent. Though the competition can boast of the same quality or even a better product, the advantage of first entrant earned the Ford Motor Company an unprecedented success.

The first entrants into the Christian faith were not so lucky. Instead, theirs was a tale of woe and agony. They paid the ultimate price for their faith. At the time when the church was to take root and blossom, Herod was stirred up to devastate the cream of fresh blood that God was about to use to spark revival in the land (Acts 6–12). Today, we enjoy their labor and expressions of liberty, paid for by their deaths and agonies. We can proudly declare that we are sons of the Most High God, without molestations or being incarcerated. It was not so with the Pharisees and the new church.

Before Saul had his first summit with God on the way to Damascus, he was an avowed enemy of the Lord Jesus Christ. After the experience, he became a different person. He was commissioned and started preaching the same gospel he had persecuted (Acts 9:1–22). Saul (later Paul) was a servant or slave of the law, culture, and traditions but was turned to a servant of God in righteousness. He was a leading spoiler of the Christian faith but later turned an avid defender of the same Christian faith. I call that repentance and conversion.

Knowing Who You Are

At Eden, our fore fathers sold our place in God. The divine nature was taken away. The Devil deceived Adam and Eve and got us into a big mess. The nature of God, resident in us, was taken away—God's character, His authority that was given, His power at work, and the mandate to dominate and rule over all things created under the earth was all taken away. Other creatures and the hemisphere became rebellious and opposed man's instructions. Man became afraid of them. Man became afraid of thunder, of earthquakes, of lions and bears, of crocodiles. He was pained to garner daily food; in pain of labor at childbirth; in pain and afraid of everything. These all came on man because the God-nature was taken away as a result of disobedience, because of sin. The glory of God was taken away. The Spirit of God was gone. The fullness of the Godhead, meant to live forever with man at creation, was no more. We then became servants of sin, prone to failures, diseases, death, and decay. What a fall from grace.

- We were servants of sin, children of the Devil, but now we have been delivered from sin and its passions (Romans 6:16–18; 7:5–6; John 8:34; 44:1; 3:8).
- We were taken captive, afflicted, and dehumanized at will by the Devil, but now have been delivered totally from the power of

darkness and translated into the kingdom of the Lord Jesus Christ (2 Timothy 2:26; Luke 13:11–16).

- We were no people, alien to the commonwealth of Israel and strangers to the covenant of promise, but have now been made sons, joint heirs with the Lord Jesus, and thus entitled to all divine blessings (Romans 9:25–26; Ephesians 2:11–16; Romans 8:17; Ephesians 1:3; 2 Peter 1:3–4; Ephesians 2:19; 1 Peter 2:9–10).
- Satan had rule and authority over us since we lost our first position due to sin. However, the new you is restored from that former position, and you now have power, dominion and authority over Satan and his cohorts (2 Timothy 2:25–26; 2 Peter 2:9; Luke 4:6; Colossians 1:20–22; Luke 10:19; James 4:7; Luke 9:1; Luke 10:1, 17).
- We were blind to the light of the glorious gospel of Jesus Christ, but now we can see (2 Corinthians 4:4).

How Does God See You Now?

God sees you as a new person entirely, someone whose sins have been washed away, forgiven, and forgotten (2 Corinthians 5:17; Galatians 6:15; Hebrews 8:12; Revelation 1:5; 1 John 1:7; Isaiah 43:25; 44:22). Sins mentioned here include all kinds of sins committed in the past. He has consequently kept you as the apple of His eye (1 Peter 2:9; Titus 2:14; Exodus 19:5–6; Deuteronomy 32:10; Zachariah 2:8; Isaiah 54:15–17).

You are a new creature that is separated to God (2 Corinthians 5:17; Ephesians 4:22–24; Colossians 1:13–14; Ephesians 6:17–18).

You are the righteousness of God by faith in Christ (Romans 3:22; Philippians 3:9; Isaiah 54:17; Galatians 2:20).

List the things that have changed in your life since you were changed from the kingdom of darkness to the kingdom of Light.

You have been saved by grace, sustained and kept by grace, no more a servant to sin but an overcomer. You are a child of the Most High God. It therefore is important that you reign and rule in dominion, occupying as He has asked you to occupy in this present world, until He comes back to take you home. I hear some puritans insist on sanctification of the body before the work of grace is considered completed. Let me say a word on sanctification.

Sanctification

To sanctify means to make holy, make pure, and to be separated to God. It is a process that starts at conversion and continues as the Christian grows into maturity. Sanctification is not the second work of grace. It does not attack and remove the root of sin; rather, it grooms the believer into a daily experience and maturity, just as though you behold your face in a mirror, from glory unto glory. With the Word of God and prayer, daily you are transformed into the image of His dear Son. God has imputed the divine nature into you (Leviticus 20:7–8; John 17:17–18; Hebrews 12:14; 2 Corinthians 6:14–18). Sanctification is not just of the body but of the soul and the spirit. Let this mind be in you which was also in Christ Jesus (Romans 12:1–2).

You are sanctified by the following ways:

- by the Word of God (John 17:17; Hebrews 4:12),
- by the blood of Jesus (Hebrews 10:19–20; 9:13–14; 1 John l:7–9), and
- by the Holy Spirit (1 Peter 1:2; 2 Thessalonians 2:13).

Conclusion

Your position is exactly like that of Saul. You were weak before but now made strong. You were an underdog to the power of evil spirits, but now you rule and have dominion over them. You are empowered to deliver men from the grip of captivity and slavery to sin.

Memory Verse

> "But ye are a chosen generation, a royal priesthood, an
> holy nation, a peculiar people; that ye should show forth
> the praises of him who hath called you out of darkness
> into his marvelous light" (1 Peter 2:9).

Notes

CHAPTER 5

Faith

"Be careful to pay attention to the things written in the
holy script, obey and live by their instructions"

What Is Faith?

Imagine this scenario: you go swimming in the shallow end of the sea and by a stroke of chance; the waves carry you farther than you imagined, into the deep. You struggle to swim ashore but cannot. In this fight for your life, there appears a big shark with sharp teeth and fierce-looking eyes. You are in its territory, alone. What would you do?

Faith is the substance of things hoped for, the evidence of things not seen. Faith is believing in an unseen yet true; in relying on and throwing all your weight into the waiting arms of God without question, without proof of validity, even with little or no knowledge of the resulting outcome of the action you are about to take. To believe is to wholly accept God's terms and go all the way, according to His instructions and directions. In the world, we prove things. We analyze (sometimes over analyze to the extent of committing analysis paralysis), and we go for what the eye can see, what the mouth can taste, and what our feelings are. Because the natural man is short-sighted and unable to see the spiritual, he is limited to programs that surround the cosmos.

To walk with God, you must have a simple, childlike trust that God is willing to save, transform, and change your life. The transformation is God-based, the foundation of the change unshaken.

1. Faith is a personal trust in Jesus Christ (Romans 4; 5:23–25; 5:1).
2. In prayer, faith is the confidence we have in God, that if we ask anything according to His will, He will hear us and answer (1 John 5:14–15).
3. Regarding unseen things, faith gives substance to those things unseen so that we act upon the conviction of their reality (Hebrews 11:1–3).
4. As a charge to man to unmask himself of the ability and skills with which man is so engrossed, as a tool for success in life, and with regard to casting everything into God's monitoring and supervision, Jesus told the disciples: "Have faith in God" (Mark 11:22–23).

Faith is the substance of things not seen and the evidence of things hoped for, but without faith, it is impossible to please God, for he who comes to God must believe that He is and that He is the rewarder of those who diligently seek Him (Hebrews 11:1, 6).

What Faith Is Not

Faith is *not* the absence of fear or of the unknown. Faith is having the fear of God, watching in awe, and being engulfed in a "wait time" to see God unfold events. Examples are Noah and Abraham (Genesis 6–9:17; Hebrews 11:7).

Faith is not always having the answer or result of your engagement as you want it. The vision beclouds what's in the physical, and results may be delayed, but faith persists—the end here justifies the means (Genesis 12:1–9; 17:1–8; Hebrews 11:8–19).

Faith is not an expulsion or absence of the five senses (sight, taste, touch or feeling, smell, hearing) but has a superimposed touch on their operations and thus affects or embellishes their limitations on the spiritual underlying fabrics, from which the physical or cosmos (on which the five senses base their theory) gain lifelines. Faith is a stretch of what the five senses cannot do.

It is not a rhetorical expression or a religious feeling. It is an indulgence.

Results are not measured by physical output only but by a total package and overall productivity index, which only God appoints. It is the currency with which you transact business with God. "For he who comes to God must believe that He is and is a rewarder of them that diligently seek Him" (Hebrews 11:6).

Faith is not the absence of pain or pressure; it is not also the absence of joy and peace.

Belief, however, is acknowledging God's supremacy. Hope is a coastline, a state of the mind, an antecedent to positive thinking about life. Faith is a substance, a catalyst, a force within; it supports the framework of the mind.

Trust is synonymous with faith. It is total reliance on God, a resignation from self-methods and style. It is total disengagement from the status quo of man and throwing one's arms and cares into the hands of God.

Levels of Faith

1. Faith that believes and introduces us into the presence of the Father
2. Faith that receives—good health, money, anointing
3. Faith that gives. When you engage in spending for your faith, it propels you to invest in the kingdom with the hope that God is faithful in rewarding you and blessing you in the future.
4. Faith that spends and is ready to be spent. Propelled by the vision, man has a mission to accomplish. He spends his life in serving and offers it as an offering for the course of Christ. He takes a step toward spending from his income or savings (outside of his tithe and offerings). He is doing this not because he is a fool but because he has seen something worth more than gold and returns from Wall Street or the stock market where he could have invested his money. He spends and is spent for the course of the kingdom of God.

5. Faith that dies. This faith says, "If perish, I perish." This fellow is dead to the flesh and has lost his self-esteem, pride, and worldly appeal to a sensual life. His grip on material things is loose and relaxed; he is ready to let go and use it for the gospel. This comes from the vision of heaven and the Lord's appearing—John 12:24–26 (the seed must die; and the way up is always down); Romans 12:1–3 (in a "living sacrifices" saga, you kill the living animal before offering it as a sacrifice); 2 Timothy 4:6–6. We see a demand from God for our lives to be poured out for His work. For the seed to germinate, it has to shed off the ectoplasm and make way for the endoplasm and nucleus of the seed (the gem cell) to come forth. The useful life allows the outer man (flesh) to die, to be subdued and tamed by the Spirit of God. Until then, the fragrance from the inner man may not ooze out to the world.

    These are the ones that catch the attention of heaven.

With eyes on heaven, undaunted by events in the world, they have a vision and are consumed by the glory that goes with it; they push on to the saving of their souls. They embrace the promise and confess that they are strangers and pilgrims on earth. They are not mindful of the country they came out of; otherwise, they would have had reasons to go back. But instead, they look for a better city, whose maker and builder is God. This is faith. Here's a testimony:

The Father's Enduring Faithfulness

As he gazed into a cloud of uncertain destination, echoes of the hind part of memory sizzled into his feverish brain. He recalled stories in folklore about an abandoned orphan. Justin Case had been asked to move to the Gold Coast, a suburban town in South Africa, to fetch some gold. His boss had provided no tools or place of habitation and nothing for sustenance or daily upkeep. He was left to fate. It was a season of trial and test. Justin kept the faith because, according to him, challenges are a test of manhood. More important, he had an unbending resolve that the result of his occupation in digging would not only lift him out of poverty but would sustain his family and his community. He resolved to go for the kill, not considering the risks and hardship, because history was about to be written, if he succeeded.

And so he left, without money, without shelter, without a relation in the Gold Coast town, and without a means of livelihood or the support of his company. It was a strange and humbling beginning. Since he had no dwelling place, the citizens of the land made a mockery him. When asked why he stayed with all the mess, Justin answered, "If they had been mindful of the city from whence they came, if they had looked back, they would have had cause to return." And so he continued to search for gold.

Soon, fate began to smile at Justin. The outcast was seen among the people. He'd hit a home run when he bought farmland far away from the reach of life (courtesy of some little savings from hard labor in the farms and cleaning and washing corpses). The owner of the farm was ignorant that the field was littered with gold, twelve feet below the upper crust. Justin suddenly became a millionaire, and grace and glamour followed.

Justin had this to say: "The Father's enduring faithfulness sustained me. His unseen hands upheld me, and I have learned that when there is a casting down, God makes for a lifting up. To Him be all glory and praise, forever and ever. Amen."

You could be the Justin of today. Don't give up; for it is the Father's good pleasure to give you the kingdom. As we celebrate today, you can count on our Father's enduring faithfulness to make you another Justin Case. May the Lord continue to lift us all up. Amen!

Faith for the Living: Some Characteristics

1. A measurable growth pattern. From milky babes at conversion, the baby grows into a meat-eater and gradually begins to associate with bone crushers. He is developing spiritual muscles and taking dominion over all disobedience to the will of God around him. Growth, to him, is unending. He is never satisfied with mediocre living and always attains the full measure of Christ until His appearing, as expected.

2. Fellowship (in Greek: *koinonia*). He enjoys having fellowship with brothers and sisters in Christ Jesus. Fellowship with other believers becomes a lifeline. He is in touch, one-on-one, not in an Internet-based community relationship. He employs and engages himself with a local church.

3. Praying with all prayers, a 24/7 commitment to communicating with God. The man that lives by faith must be a man of continuous prayer. If that sounds too old school, remember that Jesus never gave up praying. A practice on meditation on the Word of God provides an opportunity to pray always. It is possible to pray always. The man of faith prays in line with the passion of God and the program heaven has laid out for humanity. There, he prays.

4. The altar must always ooze with fresh fire (place of communion and quietness). People of African descent understand what an oracle or shrine can do to its priest if the priest is ill-prepared before he comes to appease the gods. Our God is not an oracle, but He demands absolute reverence and respect when we go to Him. The place of communion is a place of power and holiness, made with fresh anointing, which only the Father gives. To receive this anointing, the fire must fall—then we say a man has been anointed to do exploits in His church.

5. Preaching it hard. This is the testimony of your life. A receipt of the anointing guarantees a hard gospel preached against sin, Satan, and self. Preach the Word ceaselessly—at crossroads, on the highway, and in the malls.

6. Offense is a true test of faith. When offense comes, God may allow this to stay its course, because faith must be proved and tested. At such times, do not give up! Quitters never win, and winners never quit. You may be engaged in some test-taking, and God expects you to pass with distinction.

7. Living with eternity in view. One major challenge in understanding life as a journey is the imperceptible nature of our journey into eternity. We don't seem to feel the breeze whizzing past us, as we would if traveling in a car. So we think we are stationary, but there are no stationary bodies in the universe. For instance, the earth is 93.5 million miles away from the sun. It is traveling

at an unbelievable speed of 18.27 miles per second in its orbit around the sun, and at about 994 miles per hour around its own axis. The earth covers the total distance of its orbit around the sun—93.2 million miles—in one year. Who could imagine we have traveled that distance in the last one year? Just like earth, we are traveling; we are zapping through time to eternity to our inevitable rendezvous with our immortal Creator. A man of faith lives with eternity in view. He preaches with the mind-set that a day will come when God will require him to render an account of his preaching. He does business with eternity in mind, knowing that a day will be set aside to do his books of accounting and the influence of his stewardship under the business. A woman of faith sees eternity as she tends those kids under her care, as she molds their lives and teaches in the children's Sunday school. Eternity drives everything and motivates all things. As for Jesus, He endured the cross as He saw eternity. "Who for the joy set before Him, endured the cross, despised the shame …" Faith does not look at the gains of today; it captures the essence and glamour of the glory of eternity—the glory of always being with the Lord forever!

Notes

CHAPTER 6

Digging Deeper

All men who became anything in the hands of God and in His service placed a high emphasis on a personal, intimate, functional, and growing knowledge of God. Toward this enterprise, they channeled their efforts and resources in life and ministry to the pursuit of a deeper, affectionate relationship with God. It was their number-one unquenchable thirst and yearning.

For us today, there is no way to excel in Christian life and ministry except to reorder our priorities and seek a growing and deepening intimacy with God.

In this study, I will discuss the necessity of knowing God as demonstrated by our elders, whom God approved in the Scriptures. We will seek to understand the requirements and conditions that God demands in our search to know Him.

The Necessity of Knowing God
John 17:1–3; Luke 10:38–42; Mark 3:13–15

We read from Genesis 1:26–27 that God formed man in His image after a caucus meeting with the Son and Holy Ghost, indicating that the Son was fully an active participant in creation of man. Colossians 1:16

lends a voice, that in Christ Jesus, all things consist; all things were created for Him (and in Him, we move and have our being). In Him all things are jointly held, and without Him there is not anything that is made or created, yet it was necessary for Jesus to submit to the Father (Philippians 2:1–12). He learned of Him by an intimate relationship. He rose from bed early in the morning to ask for permission and to receive the power to function for the day (Mark 1:35).

In his definition of eternal life, Jesus said, "And this is eternal life, that they may know you, the only true god and Jesus Christ whom thou hast sent" (John 17:3).

We see that knowing connotes a diligent search, a self-discovery of facts, and dutiful attention to the upkeep and preservation of the pearl so received or acquired. The Bible describes the relationship between a man and his wife in this context: "Adam knew his wife, Eve."

Therefore, "to know" involves:

- an intercourse of ideas, interests, actions;
- a discovery of deep secret things in the other; and
- a fusion of hearts; one that is subsumed into the other (inseparably bonded and fused, mutually exclusive entities that now represent one organ).

Consider Mary and Martha. What does each of these characters represent?

- Latecomer with eyes at the feet of Jesus
- Very busy for God
- Smart to make wise choices; to choose the good part

In Luke 10:42, Jesus said, "One thing is needful ..." What is that one thing?

Read John 11:1, 5; 12:1–16; Luke 24:13, 29, 33.

Mary enjoyed a consistent result of being with the Lord (Mark 3:14; 2 Peter 1:2–4; 2 Corinthians 3:18).

What is God's established procedures and principles for imparting His life of power, holiness, and fruitfulness into a willing vessel?

A Lesson from Paul
Philippians 3:1–11; Galatians 1:15–19; 1 Corinthians 12:1–10; 14:19–23

Paul chose to discover the God who appeared to him on the road to Damascus (Acts 9) and laid at the feet of Jesus the supreme enterprise of knowing and discovering who He was. You remember Gamaliel, Socrates, and other men of letters who taught Paul in legal matters? Beyond the much learning and protracted involvement in civil and religious order, Paul knew that orthodox and old methods of serving God were faulted and needed to be fixed. To Paul, there was something extraordinary about the experience of the new birth. He hid himself, took up a studious incarceration, and received revelations.

If you seek God, you will find Him, especially if you seek Him diligently and earnestly.

* What really attracted Paul to seek to God above everything else? Do you think that capitalism and the quest to acquire wealth was prevalent in his time? Or was there not a show of class and feel of importance among the rich and learned?
* List options open to Paul in life that he willingly, consciously, and practically gave up in favor of the pursuit of God.

* What are the practical implications of Matthew 13:44–46?

* Do you think you found a precious pearl?

Pray that you may see this treasure and pursue to keep it with everything in you by discovering and dwelling with the Giver all the days of your life.

The Moses Experience
Exodus 33:1–3, 15–17; Hebrews 11:23–26

Knowing that God supersedes all other occupations of man, including seeking after miracles, signs, and wonders, recall that those who know their God shall be strong and do exploits; however, the Antichrist will show forth with signs and wonders, so much so that the world has never seen before (Revelation 16:14; 19:20).

Among men who could boast of their experiences and walk with God was Moses. His résumé resonates with personal experience with God and miracles to show as evidence. Moses remained the most humble, the meekest man, and a friend of God. In it all, he said:

"Now therefore I pray thee, if I have found grace in thy sight, show me now thy sight, show me now thy way, that I may know thee, that I may find grace in thy sight … I beseech thee, show me thy glory" (Exodus 33:18).

If your presence does not go with us, we'd better stay here. I pray that God may reveal to us the need to seek His glory in all things.

* Discuss Exodus 33:1–3. Can there be miracles around a work, even when God is offended and withdrawn?

* What are the characteristic resolutions of saints of old in Exodus 33:15–16?

* Have you made the presence of God the priority in your life? Such are they that find grace in His sight.

Enter King David
Psalm 27:4; 42:1–2; 63:1–8; 84:1–7

David was monarch over a whole nation. He mediated between and among families, personal lives, national issues and the temple. Cast your mind at the White House. Imagine David on the seat of power, attending to family issues. By 7:30 a.m., the secretary of state has just called to brief on a new strategy by enemies of the USA. The vice president has a meeting with him to talk about the international allies and their demands. The United Nations is asking the United States to change its sanctions against certain countries, based on national sovereignty and circular state of nations. Congress will not pass a bill on immigration reforms for fear of losing the midterm elections. The health care reform is meeting with opposition, so economic progress is diminished in the system. Just imagine the trouble for the president. In all these, he finds time to seek the Lord; he seeks the presence of almighty God.

* Can businesses and work schedules be accepted as sufficient and tenable excuses to crowd out intimate communion with God from a heart that genuinely yearns for Him?

* Compare David and Daniel. Check out the benefits that David saw in knowing God. What does Daniel say about those who know their God (Psalm 63:84; Daniel 11:31–32)?

Elijah had a personal experience. His testimony was: "As the Lord liveth, before whom I stand" (1 Kings 17:1; 18:17) What does this mean?

Elijah was able to tell to Ahab that there would not be rain for thirty months "according to my words." And at Mount Camel, he charged the prophets of Baal to call on the name of their god to come down to consume their sacrifice. "The God that answered by fire, let him be God." It takes a man who has had a close and intimate encounter with God, who has known Him and His ways and acts, to be confident in declaring such. Truly, the standing of a man before God is all the credentials needed to bring a whole nation to its knees in ministry.

* How firm is your stand on the Word of God? Do you think you have a personal revelation and conviction about what you believe and preach?

* State your conviction in a simple way:

* Do you know Him enough to act as His representative in a community where God is alien and scorned? As an ambassador of heaven, do you know the constitution of heaven and the ways of operations for its citizens? Make it plain!

John the Baptist
Luke 1:80; Matthew 11:6–9; Luke 3:1–3

John's public ministry, which God used to turn his generation around for good, lasted for about six months. He could rather have spent thirty hours waiting on God, sorting out his life toward a ministry of thirty minutes of public appearance. We must seek the Lord first for our lives. Knowing God and becoming intimate with Him guarantees all that we need to prosper in the work of the ministry. Your power and effectiveness in God's service depends on how much of God you know. The Scripture assures us, "then shall we know if we follow on to know the Lord" (Hosea 6:3).

Our boast must not be in our ability or the prosperity message that works out dollars into the ministry bank account or the great crowd that follow after us or fills the pew at every event or meeting. The tool for measurement is the personal knowledge of the Lord (Jeremiah 9:23–24) and the change that has taken place in the lives of people, a change from sinful ways to a holy lifestyle.

* What does "palace" connote in Matthew 11:6–9?

How long did John Zachariah take to prepare and seek God before his public appearance in ministry? Just try some calculations.

Basic Conditions for Knowing God

Having looked at the efficacy of knowing God in our lives, we must be willing to give whatever it takes to know the Lord personally on a daily basis. The following are conditions of which we should be mindful, as fundamental and essential to obtain:

1. New birth (John 3:3–7; 10:14–27)
   Why is new birth a very necessary condition for knowing God?

2. Intense, earnest, and total commitment (Philippians 3:7–10; Psalm 42:1–2; Jeremiah 29:13–14)
   * Is your heart dry and vague, without a spiritual hunger for His person, and you are not alarmed?
   * What could be casting a shadow between you and the Lord?

3. Humble yourself (James 4:6–8; 1 Peter 5:5–7).
   * What does it mean to be proud?
   * Why must the proud never know God?

4. Yield your neck to His yoke (Matthew 11:28–29).
   * What does this imply? Give examples.
   * Consider Moses in Exodus 20:21; 24:12–18.

5. Take heed to build your personal altars (Genesis 12:7–8; 13:14–18; Mark 1:35).
   * Build memorials. Inspect your altar daily.
   * Make the fire, and repair any damage caused by the Evil One.

6. Prompt and obedient action on the Word (James 1:19; Isaiah 66:2, 5; Matthew 7:24–27; 1 Samuel 15:22–23)
   God cannot tolerate anybody who takes His orders for granted or flaunts His instructions.

7. Come with penitence and as a baby. We must always remember that we are first children of the Most High God, saved by grace, engrafted into the commonwealth of Israel before we became anything else in the kingdom and ministry. Weep for your sins; cry for help. Blow the alarm and seek God as a child.

Look into your closed-out life (behind the scenes). Is the Lord Jesus crowded out with activities and work schedules? Has professionalism or business or the quest for acquisition of wealth alienated God from you? Do you seek Him in each step of your way? Does it look like He's distant and left in the background?

Do the right thing now: get back to where you left Him and do not go any farther without asking Him into your life right now.

Nothing, however glamorous and great, can stand as a substitute for Him in your life.

The Goat Example

The rumen of a goat acts as a big fermentation bag. Bacteria and protozoa in the rumen supply enzymes to break down the fiber in the goat's feed. This is similar to how bacteria can ferment the sugars in grape juice to make wine in wine barrels. The tiny organisms in the rumen also help to build proteins from the feed and manufacture all of the B vitamins needed by the goat. Many nutrients that help provide the goat with energy are also absorbed here. The fermentation process produces heat that helps to keep the goat warm.

Once the food particles become small enough, they pass to the second compartment, or reticulum. Here, any foreign objects that may have been accidentally swallowed with the feed settle out in the honeycomb structure of the reticulum's walls. Another name for the reticulum is the "hardware stomach."

The fermenting particles then pass on to the omasum. The omasum removes the water from them and absorbs more nutrients, called volatile fatty acids, which help supply the goat with energy.

The particles are then forced into the abomasums, or true stomach. There, the particles are digested by the stomach acid, the hydrochloric acid (HCL). This form of digestion is the same as what occurs in a human stomach. The remaining particles are then passed on to the small intestine, where most of the nutrients are absorbed by the body and made available to the goat.

To gain spiritual muscles, you must eat to your fill, just like the goat. "Eat" the Word. A constant, consistent search of truth will provide needed strength in the days of drought and weakness. A good student of the Bible searches out all truths that are preached to him or her. He or she digs to get the *rhema* out of the *logos*. He stores it in the rumen, reticulum, and omasum. He has a reservoir of food to draw from during the winter of his life. He is on a continuous "Word search," locating the truth and not selling it for any reason but instead, providing room and expanding his knowledge of his Master. For this very reason, the Lord told Elijah, "Eat enough, for the journey is far."

Find out from the following passages why we should consume the Word of God without reservation: John 1:1–12; 2 Timothy 2:15–16; John 5:39; Psalm 91; Acts 17:10–12; Jeremiah 15:16; Psalm 119:11; Psalm 1:1–3.

It All Happens When You Are Alone with God

Our passion here is to aim to win the battle without and the war within. Ask the Lord to clean your ears to hear well. Get away from the crowd, from the noise, and you'll hear God speak from His Word, or through an audible voice, or through His anointed servant.

Study the following passages: Isaiah 30:15; Psalm 27:4; Habakkuk 2:1–4; Proverbs 37:3–8, 25–40; Mark 1:35; John 8:1–2; Genesis 28:16–18; Job 1:5.

There is need to filter out the voice of God from the noise in the air. The world system is packed with noise to distract you from listening. God still speaks (Amos 3:3–7; Genesis 13; Exodus 3).

The Bible

What is the Bible?

The Bible is the spoken Word of God (Joshua 1:8). Its authority is by the Holy Spirit through the instrumentality of inspired men of old (2 Timothy 3:16–17; 2 Peter 1:20–21; Isaiah 5:11). The Bible consists of a total of sixty-six books, with thirty-nine in the Old Testament and twenty-seven in the New Testament. The Bible is the constitution of every believer. It answers every question of life, and nothing should be added or subtracted from it, as it is dangerous to do so (Deuteronomy 4:2; Revelation 22:18–19; Deuteronomy 12:32). The New Testament is the fulfillment and the perfection of the Old Testament (Matthew 5:17–19; Romans 3:31; James 2:10).

What can you learn from the Bible?

You will you discover the following from the Bible:
* Mind of God (John 1:1; Jeremiah 29:11)
* State of man (Romans 3:23)
* Way of salvation (Acts 4:12; Romans 3:24)
* Doom of sinners (Romans 6:23; Revelation 20:15; John 3:36)
* Happiness of believers (Luke 10:20; John 14:1–4)
* Light to direct you (Psalm 119:105)
* Comfort to cheer you (2 Corinthians 1:4)

* Christ is shown as grand subject (John 5:39)
* Designed for your good (Psalm 19:7–11)
* Doctrines of the Bible are holy (Psalm 19:7; Proverbs 4:20–23); true (Revelation 15:3–4; Psalm 19:8), and immutable (Hebrews 6:17–18).

What should you do with the Bible?
* Read it, to be wise (Psalm 119:98–10).
* Read it slowly, frequently, and prayerfully.
* Believe it, to be saved (Acts 16:31).
* Practice it, to be holy (Psalms 119:9).
* Mediate on it, to be successful (Joshua 1:8; Psalm 1:1–3; 1 Timothy 2:1–15).

The Trinity

Trinity means the union of three divine persons—God the Father, God the Son, and God the Holy Spirit—in one unified Godhead. The biblical foundation of the doctrine of the Trinity asserts that three divine persons bear record in heaven (1 John 5:7), and the three are one. These are the Father (John 6:27; 1 Peter 1:2), Jesus Christ (John 1:1; Titus 2:13), and the Holy Spirit (Acts 5:3–4).

The Trinity was at work during the creation of the heavens, the earth, and everything in them. Then after that, God said, "Let us make man in our image after our likeness" (Genesis 1:26). At the expulsion of Adam and Eve from the garden of Eden, God said, "Behold the man is become as one of us." So He (unity of Trinity) drove out man from the garden (Genesis 3.22–24).

When God confounded the language of man at the Tower of Babel, we see the Trinity assemble again. "Come let us [Trinity implied] go down, and there confounded their language ... So the Lord scattered them abroad" (Genesis 11:7–8).

Identify members of the Trinity at the baptism of the Lord Jesus (Matthew 3:13–17), at the baptism of believers (Matthew 28:19), and at the benediction (2 Corinthians 13:14).

The Bible says, "And without controversy. great is the mystery of godliness" (1 Timothy 3:16). The doctrine of the Trinity is a great mystery and cannot be explained exhaustively. It should, therefore, not be argued because it is a revealed truth (Deuteronomy 29:29).

The Christian life is a continuous warfare against our archenemy, Satan, the Devil. Through the fall of man, man became Satan's possession and pawn. But when we are born again, this relationship is broken. However, Satan does not give up easily; he fights desperately to regain us. The Bible tells us to resist the Devil and give him no place in our lives. We need to know about his devices to know how to curb him and frustrate his counsel concerning us.

The following is what Marie Corelli, an Italian writer of the nineteenth century, put together to describe Prince Lucio Rimanez (Satan assuming human form) in her book, *The Sorrows of Satan*:

> And as I looked straightly at him. I thought I had never seen so much beauty and intellectuality combined in an outward personality of any human being. The finely shaped head denoted both power and wisdom and was nobly poised on such shoulders as might have befitted a Hercules—the countenance was an oval, and singularly pale, this complexion intensifying the almost fiery brilliance of the full dark eyes, which had in them a curious and wonderfully attractive look of mingled myrrh and misery. The mouth was perhaps the most telling feature in this remarkable face—set in the perfect curve of beauty, it was yet firm, determined, and not too small, thus escaping effeminacy and I noted that in repose it expressed bitterness, disdain and even cruelty. But with the light of a smile upon it, it signified, or seem to signify, something more subtle than any passion to which we can give a name, an already with the rapidity of a lightening flash, I caught myself wondering what that mystic undeclared something might be. (Oxford University Press 1859, 17–18)

Some facts about the Devil

He was an archangel in heaven. His angelic name is Lucifer (Isaiah 14:12).

He was the leader of the angelic choir of God. No wonder he is leading people into perdition through music (Ezekiel 28:12–14).

He rebelled in heaven due to pride with a third part of the angels. They were sent packing from heaven (Isaiah 14:12–14; Ezekiel 28:15–17; Revelation 12:7–9; Luke 10:18). He was responsible for the first fall of man (Genesis 3:1–7). He ever remained the tempter and the accuser of the brethren (Matthew 4:1).

He is the author of sin, sickness and death (Revelation 12:10; John 10:10). He will be chained and kept in the bottomless pit for one thousand years during the millennium (Revelation 20:1–3, 10).

What are we to do to the Devil when he tries to temp us? Resist him (James 4: 7)!

Some characteristics of the Devil

God is the only self-existing one not created. God created all other spiritual beings—angels, cherubim, and seraphim and then, Satan (Ezekiel 28:13–15). Hence, like humans, Satan is a created being (Colossians 1:16). Satan is a spirit and is a personality, possessing life, intelligence, willpower, and feelings. However, being a spirit, he likes to possess a human body (with neither tail nor horn). He is a thief (Matthew 13:19; John 10:10). He is subtle (Genesis 3:1–2; Corinthians 1:3). He is a murderer and a liar (John 8:44). He is a deceiver (Revelation 12:9). He is the accuser of brethren (Revelation 12:10). He is the tempter (Matthew 4:1).

Again, Marie Corelli writes about Prince Lucio Rimanez in *Sorrows of Satan*, as Lucio delivers a letter to the protagonist, Geoffrey Tempest, from his friend John Carrington:

> Dear Geoffrey,
>
> The bearer of this [letter], Prince Rimanez, is a very distinguished scholar and gentleman, allied by descent to

one of the oldest families in Europe, or for that matter, in the world. You, as a student and lover of ancient history, will be interested to know that his ancestors were originally princes of Chaldea, who afterwards settled in Tyre—from thence they went to Etruria and there continued through many centuries, the last scion of the house being the very gifted and genial personage who, as my good friend, I have the pleasure of commending to your kindest regard. Certain troublous and overpowering circumstances have forced him into exile from his native province and deprived him of great part of his possessions, so that he is to a considerable extent a wanderer on the face of the earth, and has travelled far and seen much and has a wide experience of men and things. He is a poet and musician of great skill and though he occupies himself with the arts solely for his own amusement, I think you will find his practical knowledge of literary matters eminently useful to you in your difficult career. I must not forget to add that in all matters scientific he is an absolute master. ...

Some of the names of Satan are the Devil, Beelzebub, Beliel, adversary, dragon, and serpent. Some of his titles include the following:

In Ephesians 2:2, he is the prince of this world.
In 2 Corinthians 4:4, he is in charge of the powers of the air.
In 1 Peter 5:8, he pretends to be a lion. Whatever God does, Satan tries to copy it—he knows that Jesus is the lion of tribe of Judah. In Isaiah 4:12, however, his original name is Lucifer—son of the morning—and in Ezekiel 28:14, he is the anointed cherub.

Some believe that all people of various religions serve the same God, but at least from now, we see that there are all kinds of gods. But children of God (disciples) serve the living God (1 John 2:22).

The Antichrist (liar) denies that Jesus Christ is the Lord or the Son of God. So if you trace the origin and beliefs of certain religions, you will find out that their god is Satan.

The present location of Satan

He is at liberty to roam about the earth, but he can only be at one place at a time, with his headquarters in the air (Job 1:7; 2:2; Ephesians 2:2; Revelation 20:1–3). Satan will be chained and imprisoned for one thousand years, but it is noteworthy that he is not omnipresent.

The Ways of Satan

2 Corinthians 4:3–4

Satan deceives the unbelievers and blinds them from the truth (1 John 5:19). He manipulates those who do not belong to God, so when you engage in a discussion with unbelievers, pray against the forces operating in their lives (Galatians 1:6–9). Satan has his own preachers who are very brilliant and eloquent. Some of their preaching (satanic verses) are as follows:

"Give your life to Christ and all your problems and needs are met. You can slide your way into heaven. There are no absolutes in life. When you pray, you can access God through any and every religion. Continue in sin, and when He appears, you will be holy. Nothing is too good for the King's kid. Use everything so that your soul can prosper. Once you are saved, you forever remain saved, no matter what you do or what sin you commit. Your offering or remittance will buy you a position in the kingdom. Just come with your money!"

Doctrines of the Devil

Satan has preachers who disseminate his doctrines (1 Timothy 4:1–2). God will always supply all the needs of His children (Philippians 4:19).

Satan has his teachers who teach falsehood (2 Peter 2:1–2). They deny the virgin birth of Jesus Christ, His deity, His bodily resurrection and bodily reappearing. They preach the gospel of social needs instead of the grace of Jesus Christ. They prevent people from witnessing the grace of God and divine provision

What Does He Do to the Believers?

He accuses the Christians every moment. Anyone who is constantly doing the will of God will be accused (Revelation 12:10).

Satan is seeking the people he may devour (1 Peter 5:8). Therefore, leave no cracks in your walls so that he will not have access into your life.

He tries to lead people away by deceit, just as he did to Eve (Corinthians 11:3).

Note: We can bind all demons but we cannot bind Satan; we can only resist him (James 4:6–7). The Lord reserves the day that Satan will be bound and thrown into the bottomless pit, in judgment.

Satan's Doom

The doom of Satan is predicted in the Scriptures in Revelation 12:9–12. Satan will be uprooted from his headquarters and cast out of the earth. Satan will be chained and imprisoned for a thousand years (Revelation 20:1–3). At some point, we mistakenly pray and bind Satan. We can bind demons and resist Satan. We can forbid him to come near us (Revelation 20:7–10). Satan will be loose for a season and then cast into the lake of fire, where he will be forever (Matthew 25:41).

Prayer Points:

> ➤ Pray that God should seal every crack in your wall with the blood of Jesus; that if there is any link between you and Satan, it should be cut off you in the name of Jesus Christ.
> ➤ Pray against the operations of the Antichrist and the anti-Christian organizations. Cast out the spirit behind these operations, in Jesus' name.

Limitations of Satan
- Limited in power (Job 1:10–12; Luke 22:31–32)
- Limited in time (Revelation 12:12; Matthew 8:29)
- Limited in location (Job 1:6–7)

How to Deal with the Devil

(James 4:7, 1 Peter 5:8)
- Submit yourself to God.
- Resist the Devil.
- Be sober.
- Be vigilant.

Know Your Power
(Hebrews 2:14–18; John 11:35)

Jesus said, "I am the resurrection and the life, though Lazarus were dead, yet shall he live again." Jesus is the source of our power—nothing else! Power over death and sin lives in Him. Power over the Devil and demons are in Jesus. The knowledge of this truth sets you free, perfectly.

We were doing a crusade in Blantyre, Malawi, and witches came to disrupt the program. The power of Jesus came down. It was devastating, but tempered with mercy. Many of them confessed and yielded their lives to the Lord that night. Jesus gave them new life.

Experience the power (Luke 10:17). It is one thing to know about the power and yet another to have possession of the power and use it. This is the power of the Holy Ghost, the same power that raised Jesus up from the grave. The power of God resident in man is all that God needs to summarily deal with the Evil One and to teach him and all principalities the obedience due to God. Jesus said, I saw Satan as a lightning falling from heaven. Rejoice that your name is written in the Lamb's Book of Life.

Memory Verse
"All scripture is given by inspiration of God, and is profitable for doctrine, for reproof, for correction, for instruction in righteousness" (2 Timothy 3:16).

Notes

CHAPTER 7

Quiet Time

Genesis 28:16–18; Mark 1:35; Psalm 91; Proverbs 4:23; Isaiah 30:15

In our quest to know God and understand His ways, a great demand is placed on our lives to make room in our tight schedules so that He can speak to us. In trying to make ends meet and thus engage in spinning and winning, God keeps looking for sincere-hearted men—those whose hearts are perfect toward Him. Though God is omnipresent and omniscient and attends every secret meeting and is everywhere, there is something we must understand. God continuously searches for men and women to whom He may speak concerning humanity and the affairs of this world. There seems to be a drought of listening men these days.

It is in prayer and quiet time that God can find someone to talk to. You could be the next ear into which He wants to whisper. *Aim to win the battle and the war* —the battle of life, outside the perimeters of your home and ministry, and the war, within your home, family and ministry. There is a lot going on now. Therefore, we need to filter out the noise in the air from the voice of God. God still speaks (Amos 3:3–7; Genesis 13; Exodus 3:18–20

The main purpose of a quiet time is to have fellowship with God. God desires this fellowship, and He actually does not want a casual visit. He intends that the fellowship last forever. Therefore, a regular meeting with God is important. The purposes of the quiet time are as follows:

* To seek the face of God (Proverbs 8:17; John 4:23; Deuteronomy 4:29)
* To receive strength and be ready to attack the forces of darkness (Ephesians 6:6–12; Romans 8:31; 1 John 5:4)
* To study and meditate on the Word of God (Psalm 1:1–3; 1 Timothy 4:15–16; Joshua 1:6–8)
* To listen to God talk to us (Amos 3:7; Mark 1:35)
* For spiritual overhaul and fine-tuning (1 Corinthians 13:5)

The following excerpt from the teachings of Rick Warren is a good guide for quiet times:

• Start with the proper attitude.
• Select a specific time.
• Choose a special place.
• Follow a simple plan.

In God's eyes, why we do something is far more important than what we do. On one occasion, God told Samuel, "The Lord does not look at the things man looks at. Man looks at the outward appearance, but the Lord looks at the heart" (1 Samuel 16:7). When you come to God, you need these right attitudes.

Expectancy: Come before God with anticipation, expecting to have a good time of fellowship and receive a blessing from your time together. This is what David expected when he said, "O God, you are my God, earnestly I seek you" (Psalm 63:1; see also Psalm 42:1).

Reverence: Don't rush into God's presence, but prepare your heart by being still before Him. Let the quietness clear away the thoughts of the world. The prophet Habakkuk tells us, "The Lord is in His holy temple; let all the earth be silent before him" (Habakkuk 2:20; see also Psalm 89:7). Coming into the presence of God is not like going to a football game. He is waiting for a relationship, an uptime with His child.

Alertness: Remember that you are meeting with the Creator, the Maker of heaven and earth, and the Redeemer of humanity. Be thoroughly rested and alert. The best preparation for a morning quiet time begins the night before. Get to bed early so you can give God your full attention in the morning.

Willingness to obey: This attitude is crucial: You don't come to your quiet time to choose what you will or won't do but with the purpose of doing anything and everything God wants you to do. Jesus said, "If anyone chooses to do God's will, he will find out whether my teaching comes from God or whether I speak on my own" (John 7:17). So come to meet the Lord having already chosen to do his will no matter what.

Make a Date with Jesus!

Decide in advance when and for how long your quiet time should be. The rule is this: the ideal time is when you are at your best. Give God the best part of your day—when you are the freshest and most alert. Don't try to serve God with your leftover time. It was Jesus' own practice to rise early to pray and meet with the Father. "Very early in the morning, while it was still dark, Jesus got up, left the house, and went off to a solitary place, where he prayed" (Mark 1:35). In the Bible many godly men and women rose early to meet with God. Some of these were Abraham, Job, Jacob, Moses, Hannah, and David. The great revival among British college students in the late nineteenth century began with these historic words: "Remember the morning watch!" Think of your morning meeting with God as your morning watch. Doctors tell us breakfast is our most important meal, giving us energy, alertness, and even establishing our moods for the day. Likewise, we need a "spiritual breakfast" to start our day off right and make sure we are giving Jesus first place. We are to seek his kingdom first (Matthew 6:33).

Finally, in the morning our minds are less cluttered. Our thoughts are fresh, we are rested, and it's usually the quietest time. One mother sets her alarm clock for 4:00 a.m., has her quiet time, goes back to bed, and then rises when everyone else in the household gets up. Early morning, she explains, is the only time her house is quiet! It works for her; you need to select a time that will work for you. Whatever time you set, be consistent in it. Schedule it on your calendar; make an appointment with God as you would with anyone else. Make a date with Jesus! Then make sure you keep it at all costs. How much time you spend is a matter to be decided between you and the Lord. If a quiet time is new to you, start out slow, but aim eventually to spend not less than fifteen minutes a day with God. Out of the 168 hours we all have in a week, 1 hour 45 minutes seems terribly small when you consider that you were created to have fellowship with God.

Choose a Special Place

Where you have your quiet time is just as important as when. The Bible indicates that Abraham had a regular place where he met with God (Genesis 19:27). Jesus had a custom of praying in the garden of Gethsemane on the Mount of Olives. "Jesus went out as usual to the Mount of Olives, and his disciples followed him" (Luke 22:39).

Your place ought to be a secluded place, somewhere you can be alone, where it's quiet, and where you will not be disturbed or interrupted. This may take some ingenuity, but it is necessary. It ought to be a place:

- where you can pray aloud without disturbing others,
- where you have good lighting for reading (a desk, perhaps), and
- where you are comfortable. (Bed is not a good choice; that's too comfortable!)

Wherever you choose, make it a sacred place—a place you set aside to meet each day with the Lord and love of your life.

Follow a Simple Plan

You'll need a general plan to make your quiet time successful, but the main rule is this: keep your plan simple. Don't let it detract from your time with Christ. Below are six points for a workable quiet time. You will need the following three items:

- Bible—a contemporary translation (not a paraphrase) with good print, preferably without notes
- notebook—for writing down what the Lord shows you and for making a prayer list

- hymnbook—in case you sometimes want to sing during your praise time (see Colossians 3:16)

Relax and wait on God. Be still and quiet for a minute to put yourself in a reverent mood. Follow God's admonition: "Be still, and know that I am God" (Psalm 46:10; see also Isaiah 30:15; 40:31).

Request that God cleanse your heart and guide you into the time together. Here's a great Scripture to memorize: "Search me, O God, and know my heart; test me and know my anxious thoughts. See if there is any offensive way in me, and lead me in the way everlasting" (Psalm 139:23–24). You must be in tune with the author of the Book before you can understand what He wrote.

Read a section of the Scripture. This is where your conversation with God begins. He speaks to you through His Word, and you speak to Him in prayer.

Read your Bible … slowly—don't race through it—repeatedly, until you start to picture it in your mind. The reason some people don't get more out of their Bible reading is that they do not read this way. Remember that your goal here is not to gain information but to feed on the Word and get to know Christ better; aloud but quietly. This helps you concentrate on and understand what you're reading. Read softly enough, however, so that you don't disturb anyone. Systematically, read through one book at a time in an orderly fashion, not using the "random dip" method—a passage here, a chapter there. Read the Bible as it was written—a book or letter at a time.

To get the sweep of a book, on some occasions you may want to survey a whole book. In that case, you will read it quickly to get the sweep of the total revelation.

Reflect and remember: To have the Scriptures speak to you meaningfully, you should meditate on what you are reading and memorize verses that deeply speak to you. Meditation is seriously contemplating and rehearsing a thought over and over in your mind.

Record what God is indicating in your mind. When God speaks to you through His Word, write what you have discovered on a piece of paper. Writing it down enables you both to remember what God revealed to you and to check up on your biblical validations.

Request from God through a time of prayer: After God has spoken to you through His Word, speak to Him in prayer. This is your part of the conversation with the Lord.

Closing Thoughts

Keep your quiet time fresh with these tips:

Vary your plan. From time to time change your methods. Don't fall into the trap of performing a method instead of getting the real stuff out of the session; get to know the Christ in your study. Sometimes when prayer seems hard and heavy, spend your whole quiet time in worship (just thanking God for who He is and what He has done for you). In Psalm 145 the psalmist asked nothing for himself; he sang songs of praise to God; in the same way, sing some songs of praise to God. You can choose to lie flat on your back, meditating and thinking through Scriptures you have read, or walk the aisles, or even sit down as you study.

Spend a whole quiet time in Scripture memory. Let God speak to you in this special and charming way.

Remember, your main purpose: to get to know Christ. Don't let your quiet time become a legalistic exercise in "doing your duty." Remember that you are there to meet Jesus Christ and get to know Him better and thus be conformed to His character and lifestyle.

Need a Hearing Aid to Hear God Speak?

Truly, I don't think so. But we need to have our ears checked, cleaned out, and placed on the right frequency or signal to attract reception and audience. Our natural ear sometimes is cleaned out and moisturized for optimum performance. The same goes with our spiritual ear. As we do our quiet time, may the Lord help us to allow the spirit of God to check, clean, and transmit the right messages to us as we yield to do His will. Amen!

Quiet Time (Group Study)

Quiet time is the time set aside regularly to go to a solitary place and meet with God, to communicate with the Father through the living Word with the assistance of the Holy Spirit; also, to bring our requests to God in prayer. Through quiet time we cultivate a relationship with God. In this study I will discuss how to have effective quiet time on a daily basis with God.

Why Do We Need Quiet Time?

1. We need God's power to handle daily activities (1 Kings 19:7; John.5:5; Isaiah 40:31; Proverbs 3:5–6).
2. We pattern our lives after our Lord Jesus Christ's life by following His steps (Matthew 14:23; Mark 1:35; 6:46; 1 Peter 2:21).
3. We cultivate a personal habit of worshiping the Lord and thereby helping our personal devotion (1 Peter 2:2; Joshua 1:8; Psalm 1:1–3; 95:6).
4. We create personal adjustment to the teachings of the Bible; that is, living by the Word and reacting positively to the Bible (John 1:12–14; Matthew 4:4; Philippians 2:1; 1 Peter 2:2; James 1:21–25).
5. We develop right response to trials and temptations that confront us (1 Peter 1:3–7; Hebrews 12:10–11; James 1:2–4).

What do you require for quiet time?

1. The Holy Bible (a good reference Bible)
2. Hymnbook or songbook and dictionary
3. Notebook and pen
4. List of prayer and praise points
5. Reading or study aid (*Daily Power; Everyday with Jesus; Our Daily Bread*, etc.)

Time and Place of Quiet Time

List the time and most acceptable place for your quiet time.

Frequency: at least once a day (Daniel 6:10)
Place: a quiet place
Duration: to be determined by the believer, such that it does not encroach on another activity for the day and keeping in mind that God deserves our best, not our leftover time
Period of the day: at an acceptable time, preferably early, at the beginning and end of the day

Benefits of Early Morning Quiet Time (Please state these)

What are the benefits you have enjoyed by doing your quiet time?

- Waking thoughts are focused on God.
- Strength is received to meet the challenges of the day (Ephesians 6: 10–12).
- Great men of God, including Jesus, observed early morning quiet time (Psalm 5:3; Genesis 19:27).
- God appreciates it (Mark 1:35).

Suggestions on How to Observe Quiet Time

Begin with a short prayer asking the author, the Holy Spirit, to explain the Bible to you (Psalms 119:18). You may sing a few songs or chorus (Ephesians 5:19).

Continue to read the Bible thoughtfully, repeatedly, patiently, prayerfully, meditatively, and purposefully, providing answers to the following questions, where applicable:

- Is there an example for me to follow?
- Is there a sin to avoid?
- Is there a promise to claim?
- Is there a prayer to repeat?

- Is there a command to obey?
- Is there a verse to memorize?
- Is there an error to mark?
- Is there a challenge to face?

List areas in which the Word of God has touched you and pray on each one of them. Some of the different types of prayers that could be offered include thanksgiving, adoration, supplication, and intercession.

Maintain a balance between the time spent in prayers and study of the Bible.

Methods of Bible Study during Quiet Time

> By chapters—by topics
> By paragraphs—through bibliography
> By verses—study outlines (for example, *Daily Bread*)
> By books—*Everyday with Jesus*, for example

The methods suggested are not exhaustive. Use all the Bible study methods available at different times to avoid monotony.

Outline the Benefits of *Your* Quiet Time

- Provides an opportunity for the soul to linger in the presence of God, laying the innermost being before Him
- Provides an opportunity to enter a reverent and affectionate yet fruitful conference with God. It creates an atmosphere where God speaks to you and you speak back to Him.
- Affords a working knowledge of the Bible
- We get to know God—His nature, character and ways

How Does God Speak to You?
- By His Word (Psalm 119:105; Hebrews 1:1)
- By dreams (Joel 2:28; Job 33:14–16; Genesis 31:11; 37:5–7)
- By vision (Acts 10:3; Joel 2:28; Isaiah 6:1–4)
- The still small voice (1 Kings 19:12)

- Inward witness (Proverbs 20:27; 1 Corinthians 2:11)
- Audible voice (Acts 10:13; 1 Samuel 3:4)
- Through the gifts of the Holy Spirit: prophesy, words of wisdom, words of knowledge, etc. (1 Corinthians 14:3–4; 2 Peter 1:19)

Obstacles to Effective Quiet Time

Discuss possible obstacles to a fruitful quiet time (haste, emails, electronic promptings, bad planning, laziness, overeating, and monotony due to one method of study).

Conclusion

A fruitful and consistent quiet time brings out a balanced spiritual development in at least three different areas:

- Healthy and fruitful Bible knowledge (Psalm 119:9, 11, 105; Ephesians 3:16; 2 Timothy 2:15; Psalm 19:8; Hosea 4:6)
- Fruitful prayer life (Proverbs 15:29)
- An amiable Christian character (Matthew 5:16; 1 Peter 3:2; Philippians 3:20; 1 Peter 3:15–16)

Memory Verse

"As new born babies, desire the sincere milk of the word
that ye may grow thereby" (1 Peter 2:2).

CHAPTER 8

Touching on Water Baptism and Holy Communion

This study will look into the three types of baptism that believers might undergo. These are baptism into Christ and His body, baptism in waters (otherwise known as water baptism), and the Holy Spirit baptism.

Baptism into Christ and His Body

What does it mean to be baptized into Christ? (John 3:1–21)

Discuss 1 Corinthians 12:13; 3:27; Ephesians 4:5; 1 Corinthians 10:17.

To be baptized into Christ is to become connected with the life of Christ. This means becoming regenerated. The Holy Spirit carries out this form of baptism. The Holy Spirit "sits" on you as the preacher plants the Word of God in your heart. The Holy Spirit "cultivates" or ploughs in the

Word into your heart, and the seed begins to gain roots as you yield to the promptings of the voice of God to repent.

The Spirit again comes to help to introduce you to the Father and the Son. As you agree with Jesus, there is implantation of the seed of God. There is a heart transplant, and divine nature takes root. The Spirit begins to lead you in your new life. At this point, you develop a dislike and distaste for sin. The Holy Spirit begins to prompt you to do things right and godly. You are born again.

Water Baptism

Water baptism is an exemplification of the "real stuff"; it is likened to a receipt obtained after a purchase. Although a purchase is possible without a receipt, it is expedient that we fulfill all righteousness in getting baptized.

Identify the scriptural evidence and mode of water baptism Matthew 3:13–17; Acts 2:41; 8:12, 38; 16:33; 18:8

Must water baptism be by immersion?

The word baptism in Greek is *baptiso*, which means to submerge or immerse.

It expressed the reality of burial with Christ (Romans 6:4).

Biblical references indicate this baptism is performed in the river or a flowing canal (Matthew 3:6, 13).

In the Western world, where ice and snow prevail during winter, what options can you advise, given the weather and environmental laws with regard to rivers?

Some churches have devised a method of water baptism. Discuss the practice and where this "river" is cited in your church building.

The importance and/or significance of water baptism
- It is an outward symbol of an inward reality (genuine conversion).

- It is a symbol of identification with the death, burial, and resurrection of our Lord Jesus Christ (Romans 6:3–6).
- It is an open declaration of separation from the world.
- It is performed so that we can follow the example of the Lord Jesus Christ in fulfilling all righteousness (Matthew 3:3–15; 1 Peter 2:21; John 13:5)

In whose name should water baptism be carried out?

We are to be baptized in the name of God the Father, God the Son, and God the Holy Spirit (Matthew 28.19). The minister of God is the agent of this type of baptism.

How appropriate or scriptural is infant baptism? Discuss Acts 8:12.

The Scripture demands repentance toward God and faith toward Christ (Acts 20:21) as basic conditions for all baptism. If this is true of baptism, how can a child do this? Baptism should be performed when one is mature and able, when he understands sin and what to do to be saved. Discuss baptism in your classes.

Water baptism is an ordinance; it is a doctrine that fulfills our obedience to the Lord. It is a necessity and is done to separate us unto the Lord. It must not be placed as a yoke on believers who may, by reason of circumstance (albeit willing to be baptized), could not undergo the process of baptism. Remember the thief on the cross? He sits at the right hand of God, unbaptized. Consider those children killed by Herod, when he sought to kill baby Jesus, seated in heaven with the Father.

Holy Communion: The Lord's Supper

Holy Communion was instituted and commanded by our Lord Jesus Christ on the eve of His betrayal to all who profess Him as their Lord and Savior. It is to be observed in remembrance of Him, until after the rapture, when we shall dine with Him again in His kingdom. Hence, as Christians, we are qualified and enjoined to partake of it after we have believed (1 Corinthians 11:23–26; Matthew 26:26–29; Mark 16:16).

Who is qualified to take the Holy Communion in the church or at home (Mark 16:17; Acts 10:44; Luke 11:9–13; Acts 5:32)?

(Every obedient child of God, when required)

What does it mean to take the Holy Communion unworthily?

Why did Paul ask his hearers to first eat at home before coming to the public place on communion day?

Discuss: The reason for which a man is ineligible to take the Holy Communion is enough reason to keep him away from attaining rapture.

Validate your answer with Scriptures.

Can Holy Communion "drown" the power of sin in man's life and thus enable him to overcome?

You remember that Jesus turned water into wine at the wedding in Galilee. What kind of wine was it? What type should the church use for Holy Communion?

Memory Verse

"Therefore we are buried with Him by baptism unto
death: that like as Christ was raised up from the dead by
the glory of the Father, even so we also should walk in
newness of life" (Romans 6:4).

Notes

CHAPTER 9

Spread Like a Mustard Seed

Call to Evangelism

When Sam Walton woke up one blessed morning in 1945 in a small village in Arkansas with a dream to plant a mom-and-pop shop (a Ben Franklin franchise store) in outcast neighborhoods to help cut down prices and reach out to rural life, people took him for a joke. According to *Forbes* magazine's annual ranking of the well-to-do Americans, the heirs of Sam Walton, founder of Walmart stores, who died in April 1992, held the fifth through ninth top positions in 1993, with $4.5 billion each in asset values.

Sam Walton had built Walmart to a great success over a period of twenty years, with an average return on equity of 33 percent and a compounded average sales growth of 35 percent. By the end of 1993, Walmart had a market capitalization of $57.5 billion, with a sales per square foot of $300 (industry average then was $210). No doubt, Walmart has revolutionized retailing tactics and has spread like a California wildfire. I believe Walmart is a good case to study for the course of world evangelism, the course of spreading the gospel of our Lord Jesus Christ.

Consider the following texts: Matthew 28:15–20; Mark 16:15–18; John 20; 21; Acts 1:1–10; 13:5.

"But you shall receive power after the Holy Ghost has come upon you, and you shall be my witnesses both in Jerusalem and in all Judea and in Samaria and unto the uttermost part of the world" (Acts 1:8).

Evangelism is derived from the Greek word *evangellion* (gospel) meaning the good news. Evangelism, therefore, is the activity of the church in planting, publishing, or proclaiming the gospel to sinners, with the aim of bringing them to the saving knowledge of Jesus Christ.

Many books have been written on this subject, and they major on strategies and tactics, not neglecting the power behind the gospel. However, a mention of the scope is necessary.

Scope: The scope is the whole world with no geographical limitations, no racial or ethnic barriers, and no class distinction. This charge is not optional but is a command from the Lord Jesus Christ.

Why witness? The reasons why we must witness to others, among many others, are:

* It is a command (Mark 16:15).
* It is a wise thing to do (Proverbs 11:30).
* It brings joy and causes heaven to party (Luke 5:20).
* It adds stars on our crowns in heaven (Daniel 12:3; John 4:36).
* We are ambassadors of Christ (1 Corinthians 5:18–20).

Questions to Consider
* Why do many not witness or why are they not interested in witnessing for the Lord Jesus or even willing to defend their faith?

* Why would a Christian not engage in supporting the work of God in his or her local church? Why does he or she find it more admirable to give to other causes (being class-conscious and socially acceptable)?

* The return on investment (number of souls won to and disciples for the Lord Jesus) remains low after the end of program calculations. Why is this so? What must church leaders do to avoid this waste and misguided zeal?

The reason for the lack of laborers in the vineyard is that a lot of people in the church are not born again (transformed or changed). They have never come to experience God or asked Him to save them from their sins. They have never encountered Jesus; they are still in their old nature, despite the fact that they fill the pulpit, singing and jumping and getting excited. Handfuls are proselytes (converts from other religions into the Jewish religion) who just follow and close ranks, doing what Mom and Dad or their breadwinners insist on. They belong to the group but never were born into the family of God. And so these do not know the true God or His salvation or His mandate to evangelize the world.

I remember stories around the Azusa Street Revival in California, one hundred years ago, and the wave of revival that swept Nigeria, starting from the southeastern region after the Nigerian civil war in 1970 and spread into most African countries. It was that wave that got me into God's kingdom when we experienced the unspeakable movement of God, when the dimensions of prayer and witnessing and Bible studies were not tools for making money or for just getting among friends but were divine mandates and calls from God.

We did not seek for miracles or for the material things of this life, but we had unbending resolve to serve the God, who appeared to us and saved us from our sins and the poverty that was levied on Eastern Nigeria (a punishment for engaging in a war). Such were the experiences of those years. But today, I hear a different tune of music, different dance tactics, and thus, very different results in the church. In the beginning, it was not so designed by God.

Check Ezra 3:10–13.

"But many of the priests and Levites and Chief of the fathers, who were ancient men, that had seen the first house, when the foundation of this house was laid before their eyes, wept with a loud voice and many shouted for joy; so that the people could not discern the noise of the shout of joy from the noise of the weeping of the people: for the people shouted with a loud shout and the noise was heard afar off" (Ezra 3:12–13).

This is the major reason that has diminished the act of evangelism: the true gospel has fled from our pulpits. Preaching the gospel has become mundane and "old school," because of the craze for material things and the quest to belong to the world, along with the inertia to catch up with the prospering group and enjoy the world and its sweet offerings. It has brought the church on its knees, pleading with the world that it first led.

What, then, must we do to come back to this divine mandate? Seeing that the world has gone digital, how can we strategically refocus—even the elect and called-out ones—to the Great Commission in a more concise and targeted technique so that we might be relevant to our calling and impact our world with the gospel of our Lord Jesus Christ?

Sam Walton had two major strategies in growing Walmart to a phenomenal industry leader. The first was locating stores in isolated rural areas and small towns, usually with populations of five thousand to twenty-five thousand. According to the Harvard Business School, Walton said, "Our key strategy was to put good-sized stores into little one-horse towns that everybody else was ignoring." The store offered prices as good or better than stores in cities that were four hours away by car. The second strategy was to push from the inside out. Sam Walton had a philosophy that drove everything in business: he believed in the value of the dollar and was obsessed with keeping prices below everybody else's. His rule of the thumb on buying trips was that trip expenses should not exceed 1 percent of the purchases, which meant that sharing hotel rooms and walking instead of taking taxis formed the culture of the company.

What do we learn from this for the church?

Brand Formation and Selling Tactics

(All credits go to Goizueta Business School, Emory University)

What is a brand?

The American Marketing Association defines a brand as a name, term, sign, symbol, or design or a combination of these, intended to identify the goods or services of one seller or group of sellers and to differentiate them from those of competitors. In essence, a brand identifies the seller or maker. Whether it is a name, trademark, logo, or another symbol, a brand is essentially a seller's promise to deliver a specific set of features, benefits, and services consistently to the buyers (would-be converts).

The best brands convey quality, but the branding challenge is to develop a deep set of positive associations with the brand. Marketers must decide at which level to anchor the brand's identify. It would be a mistake to promote only one attribute.

Buyers, however, are not as interested in the brand's attributes as they are in the benefits—competitors can easily copy attributes, and today's attributes may become less desirable tomorrow. Ultimately, most enduring for the brand are its values, culture, and personality, which define the brand's essence. Smart firms, therefore, craft strategies that do not dilute the brand values and personality that have built up over the years.

Did you know that every person (or church) has a brand?

It's true. Each person or church has a unique brand. Perhaps you've already thought about this and taken the time to define your brand. If not, then you should create your brand definition immediately, because instead of defining your brand, you've let others control the message. Tell who you are.

Craft Your Brand

Values	What are the values your church lives by? What are the core values of your church? What added value does your church offer to your community?
Talents and Interests	What are your greatest talents or abilities? What interests you the most? What is your calling? (Ephesians 4:11–13)

Known For	What are you known for when people think of you?
Possible Shifts	What do you want to be known for that you are not known for now? What are your core strengths?
Future	Imagine that ten years from now, someone is describing your church to a community resident. What will he or she say?
Brand Statement	Summarize your answers to the questions above in a brief brand statement.

You are getting close to your brand

Targeted Positions	What positions are you seeking to occupy in your community (mentor, disciple, community-centered, mega-church, youth-focused)?		
Brand Description	Review your brand.		
Positioning Statement	State your selling point, your key message.		
Talent Discovery (Your key competencies)	Skills	Knowledge	Traits

Target Persons to Evangelize	Who are you more likely to win? Who are you targeting?
Price	What price are you willing to pay to get to your target audience (cost of sacrifices, monetary, and social costs to you)?
Promotion	How you are getting the word out there that your Jesus has been proved and offers the best life ever? How are you networking (seeking the help of other churches that might have more skilled workers to help leverage your efforts)? How are you learning the skills necessary to be successful in your evangelical effort? How are you learning more about your target fields and ensuring they know you? Is your program sustainable? How will you follow up?

Personal Evangelism
Group Study

Personal evangelism is a person sharing the gospel message with another person, with the aim of leading the individual to Christ. There is no greater joy than seeing a soul come to Christ. Moreover, the Bible says, "He that winneth souls is wise" (Proverbs 11:30 KJV). One of the primary reasons we are still alive after we received Christ is to be fishers of men (Matthew 4:19).

1. What is evangelism and its prerequisites?

Matthew 28:18–20; Luke 24:47; 1 Timothy 1:15; Romans 1:16; Matthew 8:5–13; Luke 9:53

2. Why must we win souls?

Ezekiel 33:7–9; Mark 16:15–16; Matthew 28:19–20; John 15:16; 14:6; 20:21–23

Why is it urgent?

John 4:35–38; Matthew 9:36–37

3. How long does it take after new birth to begin to witness to other people?

John 1:40–42; 4:25–30, 39

4. How often and where should a Christian witness?

Acts 5:42; 2:46–47; 20:20; 2 Timothy 4:2.

What are the results of these?

Acts 6:7; 19:10–11; 2 Corinthians 5:15–20

5. What things make for effective personal evangelism?

Psalm 126:5–6; Matthew 10:16

1 Corinthians 13:1–3; Luke 9:53–55; Matthew 8:5–13; 2 Corinthians 5:14; Proverbs 16:1, 16; 1 Timothy 2:1–4

6. Discuss practical problems that are likely to be met within personal evangelism.

What rewards await a faithful Christian witness?

1 Thessalonians 2:19; Daniel 12:3; 2 Timothy 4:7–8; John 15:1–2, 7–8

It is not the hearer only who will be justified but the doer of the Word. Demonstrate personal evangelism. Go out and do evangelism together with your teacher; go in pairs.

Memory Verse

> "For though I preach the gospel, I have nothing to glory
> of ... for necessity is laid upon me; yea, woe is me, if I
> preach not the gospel!" (1 Corinthians 9:16).

CHAPTER 10

Baptism of the Holy Ghost

"But ye shall receive power after that the Holy Ghost is
come upon you and ye shall be witnesses unto me both
in Jerusalem, and in all Judea and Samaria and unto the
uttermost part of the Earth"

—Acts 1:8 (KJV)

Paul having passed through the upper coasts came to
Ephesus and finding certain disciples; he said to them,
"Have ye received the Holy Ghost since ye believed?"
And they said unto him, "We have not so much as heard
whether there be any Holy Ghost."

—Acts 19:1–2 (KJV)

The Spirit of the Lord is upon me, because He hath
anointed me to preach the gospel to the poor, he
hath sent me to heal the broken-hearted, to preach
deliverance to the captives and recovering of sight to the
blind, to set at liberty them that are bruised; to preach
the acceptable year of the Lord.

—Luke 4:18–19 (KJV)

Like the experience of being born again, the "taste" of the baptism of the Holy Spirit is only at its full grip and appreciation when the recipient has a firsthand experience and the impact of His touch and soul-reengineering. Spiritual experience sometimes is beyond human expression or the passage of words, so it may be difficult to fully explain the operations of the Holy Spirit at baptism.

As the disciples gathered to worship in Acts 2, a mighty rushing wind swept the entire arena at the upper room. There was an evidence of cloven tongues of fire and speaking in the diverse native tongues of the different people and proselytes who had come to Jerusalem to worship. The people who spoke those different languages had not learned the languages but were empowered by the Holy Ghost to utter and speak languages they never had spoken. In that room, there was no laying of hands. There was understanding and meaning to the tongues spoken.

In Acts 19, Paul asked the Ephesian Christians if they were baptized in the Holy Ghost. They were not. Paul laid hands on them, and the Holy Ghost filled them up. It seems to me that the Holy Ghost has no restrictions on the way He impacts Himself on God's people. He chooses to visit in ways best suited to profit the church and glorify the Father. One thing is clear: we must all desire and thirst for His infilling and empowerment. The baptism of the Holy Ghost may be likened to a spark plug of a car. During winter, some old cars need a jump-start. In the winter season of our walk with the Master, we need a jump-start. We need the baptism of the Holy Ghost.

"And it shall come to pass, afterward, that I will pour out my spirit upon all flesh; and your sons and your daughters shall prophesy, your old men shall dream dreams, your young men shall see vision. And also upon the servants and upon the handmaids in those days will I pour out my spirit. And I will show wonders in the heavens and in the earth, blood and fire and pillars of smoke" (Joel 2:28–30).

God is mysterious. His ways are past finding. It takes a close walk with Him to experience His acts and presence. He promises to *pour out* His Spirit. The Lord means exactly what He says: "And I will show wonders in the heavens and in the earth, blood and fire and pillars of smoke."

We worshipped in a small church in Valley Estate, Dopemu Ikeja, Lagos, Nigeria. On Sunday, May 24, 1999. I was in pain because my wife was in the hospital with our new baby boy, David. Both had issues and were in the intensive care unit.

At home, my firstborn, Samuel, had caught pneumonia, and all efforts to curb the high fever yielded no results. I could see that the life of the twenty-month-old boy was ebbing out. This was May 23, 1999, a Saturday. At three o'clock Sunday morning, I put my boy in the car and drove in search of other medical help. Dr. Egejuru of Ikeja Government Reserved Area was available, and he accepted the unscheduled visit. He put Samuel on intense medications in the hospital.

In the morning, I was to preach the Word of God to the congregation. Bible study was in progress, and I went to pray in the office, but I could not pray. I wept. I told God as I cried that I had three people in serious condition in the hospital. I told God to help preserve their lives as I preached the Word. I sobbed, and my heart was heavy. Yet I had to preach that morning because no one was scheduled to preach.

I came down to the altar, and we started worship. The choir was great that morning, with songs of worship. Suddenly, the Spirit of the Lord came down. I was consumed in His presence. The ministers were with me on the altar. One of them, Minister Unemilin, came to me as I knelt and said, "Pastor, open your eyes. Open your eyes and see what is happening. Please see what is happening. There are clouds of smoke covering the whole place and the people." As I knelt and we worshipped, the clouds came. The Lord was in the clouds of smoke. Of course, miracles occurred, deliverance took place, and souls were saved.

Six weeks later, one of my ministers on the altar came forth with a testimony. He had been impotent until that day. The Lord had healed him; that night his wife conceived a baby boy. That is what the Holy Ghost can do when He visits a man or a congregation. Do you believe in miracles? Can you believe the Holy Spirit will baptize and empower you?

The Lord says, "Whosoever that seeks me, shall find me, and that early" (Proverbs 8:17).

> For thus saith the Lord, That after seventy years be accomplished at Babylon, I will visit you and perform my good word toward you, in causing you to return to this place. For I know the thoughts I think toward you,

saith the Lord, thoughts of peace and not of evil, to give you an expected end. Then shall ye call upon me, and ye shall go and pray unto me, and I will harken unto you. And ye shall seek me and find me when ye shall search for me with all your heart. And I will be found by you saith the Lord; and I will turn away your captivity and I will gather you from all the places whither I have driven you, saith the Lord; and I will bring you again into the place whence I caused you to be carried away captive. (Jeremiah 29:10–14 KJV)

"While Peter yet spake these words, the Holy Ghost fell on all them which heard the word. And they of the circumcision which believed were astonished, as many as came with Peter, because that on the Gentiles also was poured out the gift of the Holy Ghost. For they heard them speak with tongues, and magnify God" (Acts 10:44–46 KJV). How did they know that they'd received the Holy Ghost? They spoke in tongues!

God is willing to pour out and empower every Christian who sincerely comes, seeking, finding, and knocking for His gifting. The gift is not for show. The gifting of God, the baptism of the Holy Ghost, is for the building up of the church through the individual Christian. Thus, the baptism of the Holy Ghost is for the general good of the church. Immersion into the nature of God must not be taken lightly. It is God pouring Himself into man and exemplifying to the world what He can do and is about.

As a vessel, I am amazed at this infilling of the power of God, housed in a jar of clay, and nicknamed Emmanuel. I am careful to keep this clay intact and preserve it with caution, because it is subject to breaking and rotting. It is very fragile. God has chosen to pour Himself in it. That is something beyond comprehension.

It is this experience that you must desire and pursue with all the passion and indulgence. As God sees the strong desire and pursuit, He begins to do something. He baptizes you, and the pouring will know no end. Here are a few of my experiences:

Restoration '83

In November 1983 an evangelical event was put together by the Christian Union, University of Nigeria, Nsukka, Nigeria. As members, we had fasted and prayed for the move of God on campus. On the first day of the meeting at Margaret Ekpo Refectory, praise and worship went wild. Everybody was engaged in thanksgiving and worship. I was stuck at the very back of the auditorium. As we worshipped, as led by Gospel Singers International, the Holy Spirit came on me. I was alone, unhindered. God began His work. I fell flat on the floor, overwhelmed by His power, and suddenly started speaking in a tongue I never had learned. It was like an electric shock, like a current was infused throughout my body. I lay on the floor for a long time. When I was done, I knew something extraordinary had happened inside of me. Since that day, my life has turned out for good and to the glory of God.

Wahoo! It is a miracle

Sometime in 2010, I was doing volunteer chaplaincy at the West Chester Hospital in Ohio. I had completed my rounds and was headed home when I received a call from one of the nurses, asking me to come back to the hospital because there was an emergency. I went to see this man; his family—wife, daughters, and relations—were crying profusely. I almost joined in the weeping but had to call myself to order. I felt the pain right inside of me. He had cancer and needed to go to surgery immediately, but his high blood pressure stood between the doctors and surgery.

When doctors are constrained, there is hopelessness. We had prayed in the small room where family members were gathered. I started off with a song in my native language. It was a song invoking the power of God, a challenge before His name and the need for help to come speedily. We went over to see the doctors and the cancer patient. I asked the doctors to pray with me. We held hands and prayed again. As we concluded with an amen, the man's blood pressure dropped. Without wasting time, the nurses wheeled this man to the operating theater, and surgery was performed.

That man went home to spend the Christmas holidays with his family. That was the Holy Ghost at work. Next to the man's name on the screen, the hospital had written "Wahoo!" I requested they add, "It's a miracle!"

Baptism with (of/in) the Holy Spirit

The regenerating work of the Holy Spirit is different from His work at baptism. In regeneration, there is impartation of divine life or nature of God (2 Peter 1:4), but in baptism with the Holy Spirit, there is impartation of divine power for effective Christian service (Luke 24:49; Acts 1:4–5, 8; 2:1–4). Regeneration is a process; baptism is an event. It occurs, sometimes regularly. Impartation and the regeneration process establish a baseline—call it a well or reservoir—where the "event" can take place most of the time. Sometimes, the event just rests on a yielded vessel as the regenerating work of Spirit continues.

The new man is born at conversion; he takes breath from God, and a seed is planted inside of him. The divine nature involves the presence of His nature (the DNA of God) in the man. As time wanes, this nature or seed can be put to rest. In other words, He can be made to stay latent or docile and inactive. When this happens, we say this fellow is passive and nominally practices his faith. We see sin and worldliness encamp around his position as a Christian. He is unable to say no to sin and the motions of the flesh. He is easily lured into what he does not want to do.

The seed of God in him says, "This action is not good. It does not glorify the Father," but because he is weak and unable to help himself, his will is weakened. He goes ahead to please friends and colleagues; he begins to indulge in sin. The power to say no is gone. So he slides down the path of the ungodly and yields to the icy grip of satanic influences. Self is king, and the will of God in this life has waned. Within him we find the seed of God, but there is rot and decay looming over this seed, and with time, the seed is plucked and blown away by Satan. He is no more recognized among the living. He dies, spiritually.

The man infused with the power of the Spirit is like fire to the force of darkness. Instead of latency, he is aflame for his God. The empowered man is active and exudes anointing with grace. He prays with a hot passion of heaven's interests and goals. He does not need to introduce himself as a

Christian or preacher. His awe and aura ooze out radiantly; they speak for him; his character defines him and his works show who he is. God dots his path with miracles because he is the carrier of the seed of God.

The baptism of the Holy Spirit is very important to every Christian for renewed strength and as a weapon in war times. To engage in war with the Enemy, we must fight to win.

The Holy Spirit helps us to fight to win. The Lord pours out His Spirit into a man to change and remold him into a supernatural vessel. Such vessels are honorable and made fit for the Master's use in times of war against the Enemy of our souls. At baptism, the Lord also sharpens our senses and develops our spiritual connectivity. We are receptive to heavenly signals. We hear and do the things of which God approves. Our senses are sharpened and developed. Baptism also helps us to acquire some synergies directly from the Lord Almighty.

Men are naturally prey to the limiting capability of the flesh. The natural man is subject to weariness and short breaths, especially after a long day of labor. The Holy Spirit at this time enables and strengthens the weak, infusing him with some "energizer" from the inside. Man is therefore ready to carry on the assignment, even when it is obvious that the flesh is weak. This infusion of power and vigor is on the occasion of baptism by the Holy Spirit. It takes a man to experiment this assertion, to believe it. It works!

Group Study

How do you receive the Holy Spirit?

Repent and believe in Jesus for the remission of your sins. "Then Peter said unto them, Repent, and be baptized every one of you in the name of Jesus Christ for the remission of sins, and ye shall receive the gift of the Holy Ghost. For the promise is unto you, and to your children, and to all that are afar off, even as many as the Lord our God shall call" (Acts 2:38–39).

➤ Ask

"If ye then, being evil, know how to give good gifts unto your children: how much more shall your heavenly Father give the Holy Spirit to them that ask him?" (Luke 11:13).

➤ Believe

"That the blessing of Abraham might come on the Gentiles through Jesus Christ; that we might receive the promise of the Spirit through faith" (Galatians 3:14). Also: "He said unto them, Have ye received the Holy Ghost since ye believed?" (Acts 19:2).

"This only would I learn of you, Received ye the Spirit by the works of the law, or by the hearing of faith?" (Galatians 3:2).

"Neglect not the gift that is in thee, which was given thee by prophecy, with the laying on of the hands of the presbytery" (1 Timothy 4:14).

"Then laid they their hands on them, and they received the Holy Ghost" (Acts 8:17),

➤ Hearing the gospel.

While Peter yet spake these words, the Holy Ghost fell on all them which heard the word" (Acts 10:44). Remember, faith comes by hearing, and hearing of the Word of God (Romans 10:17). When you believe, you can receive (Galatians 3:14).)

➤ Act of God.

"And as I began to speak, the Holy Ghost fell on them, as on us at the beginning" (Acts 11:15).

Not everybody receives the gift in the same way. Some people do not even have to ask, and God comes down and blesses them with the gift. Others may receive when another believer (who is Spirit-filled) lays hands on them. Others may ask for the gift and thereby receive same.

1. Differentiate the baptism of, in, and by the Holy Spirit. Are there really differences among these groupings?

2. Who can be baptized?

3. What is the immediate outward sign of the Holy Spirit baptism? (Acts 2:4; 8:17; 10:44–46; 19:6–7).

4. Why is Holy Spirit baptism so important? Discuss.

    He gives power for effective and result-oriented Christian work (Acts 1:8; 2:41).

    He imparts boldness for service (Acts 2:14; 4:31; Proverbs 28:1).

    At regeneration we have Holy Spirit as "resident" in the believer, but at the Holy Spirit baptism, we have Him as the "president and commander in chief."

    The foundation is laid for the operation of gifts of the Spirit in the life of a believer (1 Corinthians 12:4–14).

5. Who should receive this baptism and when? Discuss.

6. Have you received the Holy Spirit since you believed?

7. What if your local church does not believe in the baptism of the Holy Spirit? Is any other option available for a believer?

    Pray for the baptism and have evidence and a proof. Pray for God's visitation and empowerment. Taste and see. Do not argue. Prove the experience today!

Notes

CHAPTER 11

Christian Conduct

The transformed man has the divine nature of God (the seed of God) inside of him. This nature blossoms and radiates freely to the outside world as he continues to live under this consciousness and understanding. The character and values of a child of God are not meant to diminish but to grow into more of Christlike nature, from glory to glory.

In all societies and communities, there are sets of governing rules and regulations. The same goes with the kingdom of God. The Bible, the kingdom's constitution and manual, gives a code of conduct, which is a guiding light for all Christians to wholly identify with.

Character and Values

Character is the attitudinal manifestation in a life, summed up in the fruit of the Holy Spirit as it shows forth in daily activities and behavioral exchanges. Values, however, are ideals, inner linings of premeditated self-taught doctrines. They form the DNA of a man that manifests in form of character.

Character is behavioral leverage that manifests at points of decision in our daily engagements and activities. Character is the meat in the meal of life; it offers itself as a baseline before God and men as we present anything to those who listen to us. Therefore, character and values are a necessary trait as we live and preach the gospel of Jesus Christ.

In this study, we will examine the Bible-accepted ways of behaving, need-to-know models, and practical approaches to living a fruitful life.

> Through the knowledge of Him that hath called us to glory and virtue: whereby are given unto us exceeding great and precious promises; that by these ye might be partakers of the divine nature, having escaped the corruption that is in the world through lust. And beside this, giving all diligence, add to your faith virtue, and to virtue knowledge; and to knowledge temperance, and to temperance patience and to patience godliness; And to godliness brotherly kindness and to brotherly kindness charity. For if these things be in you and abound, they make you that ye shall neither be barren nor unfruitful in the knowledge of our Lord Jesus Christ. (2 Peter 1:3–8)

Faith	yields to	Virtue
Virtue	yields to	Knowledge
Knowledge	yields to	Temperance
Temperance	yields to	Patience
Patience	yields to	Godliness
Godliness	yields to	Brotherly kindness
Brotherly kindness	yields to	Charity

Explain this model in a simple, easy-to-understand way.

Examples of Bad Behaviors: ***Temple Etiquette***
1. Uzi: on helping the ark from falling. (Using your five senses in the work of the Lord is bad.) Ask God to lead in His work.
2. Sons of Aaron (Numbers 10:1–10): offering strange fires. Overstepping your boundaries in the discharge of certain duties and assignments in the temple
3. Ananias and Sapphire (Acts 5): lying and showing off to the Holy Spirit
4. Sons of Eli (1 Samuel 1): cheating, fornication, swindling
5. Hezekiah (Isaiah 38:1–5; 39:1–8): disclosure of the secrets of the temple
6. Belshazzar (Daniel 5:1–6; 26–30): desecration of holy vessels
7. Chewing gum during worship service
8. Walking about during worship service
9. Answering or making calls in the church during worship service
10. Gathering at nursing stations for a chat during worship in the name of feeding the baby
11. Littering the church (a "this is not my home" attitude)
12. Passing by without fixing something that is broken or littering
13. Drinking and eating in the sanctuary
14. Trading (buying and selling) in the sanctuary
15. Arriving late to church and having a carefree attitude toward it
16. Forming another meeting or discussion outside the church meeting
17. Disrespecting the Holy Spirit (walking about during prayers, looking around when one should be praying)
18. Being too familiar with God (chewing gum, texting, answering calls during worship service)
19. Absence of fear and sense of worship at church or other revered places of worship
20. Lack of home training displayed in public places

What must the church do to bring a change?

Other Attitudes That Affect the People

Malice: Malice can be defined as having a desire to harm others or having ill will toward others. Malice is an aberration to any child of God; therefore, put it away (Ephesians 4:31–32). Lay it aside (1 Peter 2:1). Put it off (Colossians 3:8). Restore relationships immediately with anyone who you have shown malice.

Against who do you have a grudge?

Write down what you should do from this point forward.

Strife: Strife is contending or struggling with people of opposing views. It seldom is accompanied by hot and abusive words. The regenerated man should not live with this manner.

Read 2 Timothy 2:24 and Philippians 2:3–11.

Strife leads to uncontrollable situations (Proverbs 17:14; 26:17).

It is an honor for a man to refrain from strife (Proverbs 20:3; Titus 3:9).

We should follow the example of Jesus Christ, who did nothing through strife or vainglory. At the end of His ministry here on earth, God highly exalted Him and gave Him a name that is above every other name (Philippians 3:3–11). If you experience strife with people in your workplace or school or neighborhood, you are still carnal (1 Corinthians 3:3; 6:6).

Envy/Jealousy: It is the grief, annoyance, or depravity one feels at the joy, happiness, or good fortune of another person. In the heart of a jealous person, it says, "I am better suited for that good stuff. Why should he be the one to have it?"

Outline how envy showed up in these lives:

Cain (Genesis 4:3–9)

Saul (1 Samuel 18:7–9)

Pharisees (Matthew 13:55–57)

The high priest (Acts 5:12–18)

Envy and jealousy often arise when we desire to have what belongs to someone else (2 Corinthians 10:12). This could be a position at the workplace, money, physical or spiritual gifts, recognition, or relationships. You feel that recipient is not worth the benefit; that you are a better candidate for it. In your eyes, that fellow is despised. If this is allowed to continue, it can breed hatred and malice. Please read Hebrews 12:1 and Psalm 121:1. Check out how John the Baptist handled jealousy rightly in John 3:25–27.

What did he do?

Anger: Anger is a momentary insanity displayed at the pleasure of having one's way. The Bible regards a person who is easily angry as foolish (Ecclesiastics. 7:9). Words spoken and actions taken in anger, even with seemingly genuine reasons for anger, are often done without deep thought and could derail God's plan for us, as it did for Moses (Psalm 106:32–33). This is because the wrath of man and God's righteousness are not compatible (James 1:20; Proverbs 19:19). You probably have heard people say, "That's my nature. That's me. You cannot change it." Do not accept anger or bad temper as your nature (2 Peter 1:4). A person who calls himself to order is wise (Proverbs 16:32; 19:11). Jesus even had reason to be angry, but He did not act on it (Matthew 11:19; 26:27; Mark 3:21; John 7:20; 18:30).

What are the panaceas for anger?

What can you employ as a strategy toward curbing unnecessary anger?

Write the names of the casualties that are the result of your anger. Call these folks and apologize today.

Unforgiveness: The Bible regards a person with an unforgiving spirit as wicked (Matthew 18:23–35; Isaiah 3:11). Inability to forgive others has many side effects, such as bitterness and revenge (2 Samuel 13:20–28), hindrances to prayer (Mark 11:25–26), and exposure to the Devil (Matthew 18:34), who could bring affliction or open you to other sins. This could make you indifferent or happy when other people are suffering or in pain (2 Samuel 16:5–8). You must also forgive yourself after repentance, as you cannot be more grieved than God over sins committed. Take time now to identify those you have hurt and those you have not forgiven (Colossians 3:13; Ephesians 4:32). Do not allow another person's sinful nature to hinder you from focusing on heaven. Unforgiveness is naturally followed by revenge.

Forgiving someone can be difficult. Why?

Why do we need to forgive others?

How can we forgive someone?

Forgiveness is not only about others but about our own spiritual growth. Love and forgiveness cannot be separated. If we choose to live out the love of God as the purpose of our lives, then forgiving is an option that cannot be avoided. (Please read *The Bait of Satan* by John Bevere.)

Gossip: Gossip is idle talk or spreading rumors about others. It is seeking or revealing information about the behavior and personal lives of other people.

Very few Christians own up to this venom that destroys God's people (Numbers 12:1). The consequences of engaging in gossip include betrayal of confidence (Proverbs 11:1), character assassination (Proverbs 18:8), separation of friends (Proverbs 16:28), and revealing problems to fellow men that they should discuss with God alone (1 Timothy 5:13).

My name is Gossip.
I have no respect for justice.
I maim without killing.

I break hearts and ruin lives.

I am cunning and malicious and gather strength with age.

The more I am quoted the more I am believed.

I flourish at every level of society, including churches.

My victims are helpless.

They cannot protect themselves against me because I have no name and no face.

To track me down is impossible.

The harder you try, the more elusive I become.

I am nobody's friend.

Once I tarnish a reputation, it is never the same.

I topple governments and ruin marriages.

I ruin careers and cause sleepless nights, heartache, and indigestion.

I spawn suspicion and generate grief.

I make innocent people cry in their pillows.

Even my name hisses.

I am called gossip,

—Anonymous

Think before you repeat or "transmit" the story. Ask yourself, "Is it true? What is the source, and how true is the story? Does the story help advance the course of humanity? Is it inspiring? Does it apply grace to the spirit of men? Is it necessary? Does the story meet the need of someone for the moment? Is it kind? Can it be repeated to the person about whom the story involves?

Here is a story my grandpa told me:

A baby guinea fowl came by as a chicken was being dissected and sliced into pieces. She stood with wings akimbo, laughing. The mother guinea fowl flew by and rebuked the baby, saying, "As you watch the chicken dissected and sliced, so shall men dissect and slice you. As we of the species are prone to the same passage of time, your day will come—and that will be soon—when you will be on that butcher table. Men will catch you and do to you as they are doing to your peer. So, my child, do not rejoice when your friend or even your enemy is dissected and sliced. Instead, take note that men will use the same knife and do the same job on you."

Do not give your ear to a gossip, or pay attention to it, or lend your time to stories that destroy a person's character, because one of these days, someone will tell another person your story, with "sweeteners" added.

Stealing: Stealing is taking possession of whatever does not belong to you. Examples in the Bible of those who stole are Rachael (Genesis. 31:19), Judas (John 12:4–6), and Onesimus (Philemon 1:10–16). One can steal from God (Malachi 3:8) or from parents (Proverbs 28:24). One can steal employees' wages (Leviticus 19:13; James 5:4) or the employer's time and property. A thief is under a curse (Zechariah 5:1–4). He shares a common name with the Devil (John 10:10a); he is destined to be destroyed (Proverbs 21:17). If you are involved in stealing under whatever name, repent today (Ephesians 4:28) as Onesimus did, because no thief will be found in heaven (1 Corinthians 6:10).

Stealing from God

1. What does the last of the Ten Commandments warn us against doing? (Exodus 20:17). Thou shalt not ......
2. How does the power of the gospel help us in our thinking? (2 Corinthians 10:4–5). It can bring every ..... into obedience.
3. How does the Bible say our thoughts affect what we do? (Luke 6:45). Out of the thoughts in our hearts (minds) we ......
4. What does the eighth commandment say? (Exodus 20:15). We should not ...... "Thou shalt not steal." What about stealing the members of another church? Cite examples: .....
5. When we are not treated fairly, what does God tell us to wait for? (James 5:7). Unto the .... of the Lord. How could you start your own ministry out of anger? ....
6. How are we stealing from God? (Malachi 3:8). In ....and ....
7. What portion of our money does God claim? (Leviticus 27:30). All the ....
8. What is meant by tithe? (Leviticus 27:32). ....

9. From where do we get the ability to make money? (Deuteronomy 8:18). From ....

10. Who owns the world and everything in it? (Psalm 50:7, 10–12). ....owns it all. Does God really need the money?

11. Specifically, to whom does the money belong? (Haggai 2:8). To ....What projects are they applied to

    (a)

    (b)

    (c)

    (d)

    (e)

12. In ancient Israel, who received the tithe? (Hebrews 7:5). The sons of .... In our day, who receives tithe? ....

13. Tithing in the New Testament: How does God plan for the support of the preaching of the gospel today? (1 Corinthians 9:13–14). They are to live of the

14. Did Jesus recognize the tithing principle? (Luke 11:42). These ought ye to have

15. In what spirit are we to return our tithes and offerings? (2 Corinthians 9:7). Complete this: God .... a cheerful ....

16. Where is the only truly safe place that we can put our money? (Matthew 6:19–20). Lay up for yourselves ....in............

17. How do our giving habits affect us? (Matthew 6:21). There will your .... be. The day of your tears (Psalm 20). How?

18. How do we show that we have the love of God in us? (1 John 2:5).
    If we ....His Word.
19. When we share our means to help those less fortunate than ourselves, to whom does Jesus consider the gift to have been given? (Matthew 25:34–40). We have done it unto
20. What has God promised to do for those who remember to return their tithes? (Malachi 3:10). He will

Stealing from Man

1. Mention ways we steal from government.

2. Because stolen bread is sweet, what justifications do people have when faced with falsification of records

3. List the consequences of stealing in our society

4. How do men swindle others and feel very comfortable?

What is God's judgment for those who take what does not belong to them?

Stealing from Yourself

1. How do you steal from yourself?

2. From Proverbs 11:22–23, provide solution for the curse imposed by the people.

3. Acts 20:38 provides …

4. Luke 6:38 makes certain provisions, such as …

5. 5.What do you stand to lose from not obeying these Scriptures?

Pride: Pride does not exist in isolation. There is usually a feed to the nature and display of pride. Competition and comparisons lead to the notion of feeling more important than or superior to the other person. It gives us a sense of exaggerated worth or importance. Because of the rift or vacuum in which the self-centered man lives, he begins to compare or compete to establish something that was lacking; thus, pride sets in.

Pride in another person is not necessarily evil; we should be proud of those who are steadfast in God's will and work (1 Corinthians 5:12, 2 Corinthians 7:4; 8:24).

You can be proud of someone else and still be in God's will. You can be proud of your son, daughter, or spouse, and even your country.

When we are outside of God's will, we can take pride in what is seen (the physical aspects of life) as opposed to the spiritual. Pride is portrayed in the Bible as a necklace, a crown, and fruit. The Bible also says that pride persecutes (causes pain), deceives, and brings low. It's often seen as the first sin.

The sin of pride made the Devil fall from his privileged position as an angel of light. The Devil then used the same sin to tempt Adam and Eve away from their fellowship with almighty God. Satan still tempts us today with the sin of pride.

"There is one vice of which no man in the world is free, which everyone in the world loathes when he sees it in someone else; and of which hardly any people, except Christians, ever imagine they are guilty themselves."—C. S. Lewis on the sin of pride in his work, *Mere Christianity.*

Here are a few examples of the sources of a man's pride: heart, appearance, wealth, power, nationality, ethnicity, education, beauty, spiritual gift, ministry positions or office.

Name other sources of pride

In your own words and understanding, answer these questions:
• What is pride?

• What does God say about pride?

• What are the consequences of this sin?

• What can we do about it?

Pride occurs when you hold a high opinion of yourself or achievements. It is also the actions (in thoughts, words, or deeds) you exhibit because of the relative advantage you have over others (Jeremiah 9:23–24).

Some biblical examples include Satan (Isaiah 14:12–16), Goliath (Isaiah 17:42–44; 49–50), Nebuchadnezzar (Daniel 4:30–33), Herod (Acts 12:21–23), and Ahitophel (2 Samuel 16:23; 17:23).

Pride comes with undesirable consequences—destruction (Proverbs 16:18), an ingredient in every quarrel (Proverbs 13:10); self-dependence (Psalm 10:4); keeping a distance from God (Psalm 138:6); an abomination to God (Proverbs 16:6–7); frustration in life (James 4:6); rejection of God's Word (Jeremiah 43:2).

If you want to be free from pride you must address your heart and identify with the mind of Christ (Philippians 2:5–11). You must recognize God as the ultimate giver (John 3:27; 1 Corinthians 4:7). Cultivate a humble spirit (Matthew 3:11; Philippians 3:4–10; Acts 3:12) Prefer others in love (Philippians 2:3).

"Mark this: There will be terrible times in the last days. People will be lovers of themselves, lovers of money, boastful, proud, abusive, disobedient to their parents, ungrateful, unholy, without love, unforgiving, slanderous, without self-control, brutal, not lovers of the good, treacherous, rash, conceited, lovers of pleasure rather than lovers of God, having a form of godliness but denying its power. Have nothing to do with them" (2 Timothy 3–5).

"Do not love the world or anything in the world. If anyone loves the world, the love of the Father is not in him. For everything in the world-the cravings of sinful man, the lust of his eyes and the boasting of what he has and does-comes not from the Father but from the world. The world and its desires pass away, but the man who does the will of God lives forever" (1 John 2:15–17).

Pride:
1. It is sin.
2. It relies on competition or comparing one to another.
3. Christians may be spiritually proud, condemning other people.
4. Everyone is tempted with the sin of pride.
5. Servant leadership is the model Christ portrayed for us.

Our attitude toward pride, according to Philippians 2:5–11, should be the same as that of Christ Jesus.

Worry

"Be anxious for nothing, but in everything by prayer and supplication, with thanksgiving, let your requests be made known to God; and the peace of God, which surpasses all understanding, will guard your hearts and minds through Christ Jesus" (Philippians 4:6–7 NKJV).

Consider these quotes:

"When I look back on all these worries, I remember the story of the old man who said on his deathbed that he had had many troubles in his life, most of which had never happened."—Winston Churchill, British Prime Minister

"Let us be of good cheer, remembering that the misfortunes hardest to bear are those which will never happen."—James Russell Lowell, American poet and diplomat

What is a primary cause of anxiety?

There is a right and healthy fear. The fear of the physical harm and the fear of the spiritual being (God) who keeps us safe and sustains our lives is the right fear. When our minds focus on improper fear (being fretful or frightened) of physical things, rather than reverence and awe of God, worry is the result. Also, when we allow our minds to focus on doubts and uncertainties, we become anxious. "Fear has torment" (1 John 4:18).

Can our actions or lack or actions give us things to worry about as well?

One cause of anxiety is foolish, imprudent, or evil (sinful) behavior. The Scriptures counsel us to employ foresight to stay away from such actions. When we obey and stay away, that helps us to avoid much worry.

Is anxiety caused only by "wrong" thoughts and actions? If this is so, how can we tame or eradicate these thoughts and actions?

How do we create a balance with regard to the following Scriptures? "The soul of a lazy man desires, and has nothing; but the soul of the diligent shall be made rich" (Proverbs 13:4), and "Do not overwork to be rich; because of your own understanding, cease!" (Proverbs 23:4).

Finally, let us consider friendly advice from the Lord Jesus Christ:

> Then He said to His disciples, "Therefore I say to you, do not worry about your life, what you will eat; nor about the body, what you will put on. Life is more than food, and the body is more than clothing. Consider the ravens, for they neither sow nor reap, which have neither storehouse nor barn; and God feeds them. Of how much more value are you than the birds? And which of you by worrying can add one cubit to his stature? If you then are not able to do the least, why are you anxious for the rest? Consider the lilies, how they grow: they neither toil nor spin; and yet I say to you, even Solomon in all his glory was not arrayed like one of these. If then God so clothes the grass, which today is in the field and tomorrow is thrown into the oven, how much more will He clothe you, O you of little faith? And do not seek what you should eat or what you should drink, nor have an anxious mind. For all these things the nations of the world seek after, and your Father knows that you need these things. But seek the kingdom of God, and all these things shall be added to you." (Luke 12:22–31)

If there is nothing to be gained from anxiety, how would you model your life to live without it?

Notes

CHAPTER 12

Christian Discipline

Discipline is a training that is expected to produce a specific character or pattern of behavior. It produces moral and mental accent and controls the behavior of individual, which produces a systematic, enduring way of life. It is based on submission to a set of rules and authority.

Discipline also may be defined as the training of the mind and body to produce self-control, orderliness, obedience, and capacity for cooperation. In the army, a soldier is expected to be disciplined and to distinguish himself from civilians. In the same manner, a Christian, as a soldier of Christ (2 Timothy 2:3–4,) is expected to be disciplined and to behave differently from unbelievers.

The most basic challenge that people face is acceptance. People fail to accurately perceive and accept their present situations or very often, they blame their misfortunes on other people. It is important to identify an area where your discipline is weakest. Assess your abilities and shortfalls right now. Acknowledge and accept your starting point, and design a program for yourself to improve these areas.

Acceptance means that you perceive reality accurately and consciously acknowledge what you perceive. Then, work toward a corrective action. A basic mistake regarding self-discipline is people's failure to accurately perceive and accept their present situation. Seldom do people engage in correcting what has been marred in their character or seek help to fix it, but we are encouraged to do so.

Christian Discipline

Practically discuss how a Christian should discipline himself with regard to using his tongue (James 3:2–10).

> *"Self-discipline is like a muscle: the more you stretch and train it, the stronger and more elastic it becomes. The less you train it, the weaker it becomes"*

The tongue can be used positively to offer praises and prayer to God (James 5:13), preach the Word (James 5:10), or confess sins or faith to God (1 John 1:19; 2 Kings 4:25–26). Confession could be regarding salvation (Romans 10:16) or turning adverse situations around (Proverbs 15:1). It also could be used negatively to curse men (James 3:9b), to complain (James 5:9), and to swear (James 5:12).

What does your tongue do? Boast? Is it a wall of fire? Is it an unruly evil full of deadly poison? Was your tongue used to bless someone or to glorify the Lord or in an act of worship?

When last did you use the words 'please' or 'thank you'?

Words take their root from the heart. (Matthew 15:18; 12:34b). A man not born again has an unregenerate heart (Jeremiah 17:9) and therefore an unregenerate tongue. The Bible enjoins us to be careful about the state of our hearts (Proverbs 4:23), because that determines our fate and what we say (Matthew 12:37).

> *"Willpower is your ability to set a course of action and engage in a concentrated effort. It requires gathering all energies and making a positive thrust forward. It is the ability to gather the inner strength and make a decision or take action. In the process, set goals and tasks are executed, regardless of inner and outer resistance, discomfort, or difficulties."*

"The difference between a successful person and others is not a lack of strength, not a lack of knowledge, but rather a lack of will."—Vince Lombardi

Moderation: Practice moderation in all things—eating, sleeping, dressing, spending, driving speed (Philippians 3:19; 4:5; Proverbs 20:13; 23:21; 1Timothy 2:9; Deuteronomy 22:5).

How moderate is your moderation?

Indebtedness to Money (Romans 13:7–8; Deuteronomy 28:13)

How much do you owe on your credit cards?

Promise or Vows (Psalm 105:7, 10; Ecclesiastics 5:2–5; Numbers 30:2)
Did you fulfill or pay your vows to the Lord?

Time (Ecclesiastics 3:1–8; 9:10)
How do you plan your time? Does your family suffer at the expense of your ministry or job?

Preaching the Gospel (1 Corinthians 9:16–17; 2 Timothy 4:12; Romans 1:16)
When did you last go out for personal witnessing or engage with someone to share your faith?

Punctuality, Self-Control, Orderliness at Meetings (1 Corinthians 14:40)

If the president invited you to come to the White House on a Monday at 9:30 a.m., how early would you start to prepare? When God (and His church) agrees to meet with you on Sundays at 9:00 a.m., what is your attitude toward tardiness or refusal to meet with Him?

When you go for a meeting and you are provided with free food, how do you behave?

As you walk into the church of God, temple etiquette demands that you are orderly. How often have you engaged in texting or surfing the web as the sermon goes on?

Chewing gum, walking about unruly or letting kids run in the aisles—stop this disorderliness. You vex the Holy Spirit!

Self-discipline is the ability to get yourself into action, regardless of your emotional state. This is the energy that brings the will under control, training it to be better in executing a task or managing a process. Self-discipline is like a muscle: the more you train it, the stronger it becomes. The less you train it, the weaker it becomes.

Diligence in Work—attention to details; doing your work with energy and dedication (Proverbs 22:29; 24:30–31; 2 Thessalonians 3:10)

Respect—for one another, especially pastors, preachers, ministers, and leaders in the church (1 Timothy 5:1–2, 17; Hebrews 13:17; Leviticus 19:32)

Persistence is the ability to go on in the face of discouragements. It is an action taken regardless of feelings or hostile overtures from peers or friends. Persistence allows you to keep taking action, even when you don't feel motivated to do so, and thus, results may not be seen immediately. A persistent man sees the overall picture of things to come. "It is required in stewardship that a man is found faithful."

Respect for parents and the law of the land (Ephesians 6:1–3; Matthew 15:4; 1 Peter 2:13–17; Titus 3:1)

Rebellion, especially against church leaders (Number 12:1–10; 16:1–5, 28–33; Hebrews 13:17; Joshua 1:16–18; 2 Peter 2:10–13)

Visiting nightclubs, unruly joints, wild partying, watching TV channels that do not edify (2 Timothy 2:19–21; 1 Thessalonians 5:22; 1 Peter 4:3; Ephesians 5:11–12)

Where did you go to, last Friday or Saturday night? What did you watch on TV?

God watches our private activities. He knows everything that we do in secret.

Self-discipline becomes very powerful when combined with passion, goal-setting, planning, execution, monitoring, follow-up, and sustainment.

"Discipline
This is the strength of the inner will; of being able to
behave and work in a controlled way that involves
obeying particular rules, orders or standards"

Hard Work—this is diligently and habitually engaging in a task (sometimes for long hours) and getting the assigned task completed on time. "The big secret in life is that there is no big secret. Whatever your goal, you can get there if you're willing to work."—Oprah Winfrey

Industry is working hard and working smart. It is developing the capacity to put in the time where it's needed and to do it correctly. It involves devising tactics to solve life's problems; it is diligent discovery and the application of styles and values toward accomplishing goals and tasks. Industry is developing the capacity to put in the time and effort.

Conclusion

By doing things "decently and in order" in the church, we show proof that our salvation is real and genuine—a quality product that is coming from a seed planted by the Father. "Show me your faith, and I will show you my faith with my works"—James, Jesus' brother (James 2:18).

Memory Verse

> "Let your moderation be known unto all men. The Lord
> is at hand" (Philippians 4:5).

Notes

CHAPTER 13

Fasting and Praying

Obesity and overeating continue to plague our society, with so much to worry about in the health management of our people. Stress, hopelessness, and anxiety all combine to attack our minds and our physiques. Most often, we redefine the battle and make it against ourselves, finding solace in an uncontrolled eating habit and thus becoming overweight. Christians, as well as those of other faiths, engage in fast. Fasting is abstaining from food (and sometimes, water) for a specific time, within which a certain spiritual "project" is planned and executed. Christian fasting is performed together with prayers; otherwise, it would be a weight-loss exercise or an act of abstinence without recourse to a spiritual project.

"But I keep under my body, and bring it into subjection" (1Corinthians 9:27)

What is fasting?

Fasting means abstinence, and biblical fasting means abstaining from food and drink for a period. Thus, fasting is an act of denying ourselves things that give us pleasure, toward suppressing the flesh and uplifting the spirit. A few people live a life of fasting and prayer; others fast as need arise and therefore focus on a specific prayer plan and purpose. Whichever is the case, Christians ought to fast, always knowing that Satan, our accuser, seldom wants us to live a victorious lifestyle. To gain traction and momentum, we must fast and pray.

Fasting could be categorized as follows:

> Absolute fast: abstinence from food and water for a stipulated time. After three days, it is medically advisable to drink water.

> Normal fast: we can take a meal after twenty-four hours, but water may be taken before that, depending on the duration of the fast.

Who should fast?

> Individual believers (2 Samuel 12:16; 2 Corinthians 6:5; 11:27)
> Groups of believers (Acts 13:1–3)
> A whole nation (Jonah 3:5–9; Esther 4:15–17)

What will you achieve by engaging in fasting and praying? (Isaiah 58:6–9).

The Purpose of Fasting and Praying

Below, find a table that specifically outlines the primary reasons why we must fast and pray. There may be other reasons, contingent on our personal needs, but the Lord asks us to do the following:

Practically state what must be done in each column (Isaiah 58:1–8)

1. To lose the bands of wickedness	verse 6	
2. To undo the heavy burdens	verse 6	
3. To let the oppressed go free	verse 6	
4. To break every yoke	verse 6	
5. To give bread to the hungry	verse 7	
6. To restore the poor	verse 7	
7. To clothe the naked	verse 7	
8. Not to hide from relatives who need our help	verse 7	

All these could be summarized in James 1:27. Regardless of whether you are fasting, you are expected to lead a life of practical daily holiness (1 Peter 1:15–16).

When you fast (not *if* you fast), what is the premeditated mind-set toward this effort? What drives you?

On the day you set out to fast and pray, do friends and relatives seem to offer the best meals for free or the day the aroma from a fast-food joint smells the best, offering a warm welcome?

What strategies do you employ to overcome the temptation not to eat then?

Keep a prayer journal. Use this format when you fast and pray.

Date Prayed	Prayer Points	Back-up Scriptures	Date Answered

Do not forget that answers to prayer from the Lord could be any of the following:

Granted (yes, you have it);
Wait (until the time is right), or
No (I will not grant that request—this is usually for our own good and continuous blessings from the Father).

Mention some other strategies you may employ while fasting and praying.

Other Advantages of Fasting

It puts down our flesh and increases our spiritual sensitivity, strength, and awareness. "But they that wait upon the Lord shall renew their strength" (Isaiah 40:31; Psalm 35:13).

It makes clearer the purpose of God in our situations as we become more receptive in the spirit.

We possess keener perception of divine things and clarity of thought.

Fasting helps to kindle and develop faith. Through fasting, spiritual fire is nurtured and faith operates well.

It helps break the power of Satan, which leads to deliverance and healing (Mark 9:28–29).

It improves prayer life tremendously (Luke 11:9–11).

It enhances continuous flow of anointing.

When Should We Fast?

- When asking for divine secrets (Daniel 9:3, 20–22; 10:2–3)
- When in danger (Acts 27:21–25; Jonah 1:17; 2:1)
- When making a crucial decision (Esther 4:15–16)
- When sick and in need of deliverance (2 Chronicles 7:14)
- When preparing for a great task or revival (Matthew 4:1–3)
- When asking God for intervention (Nehemiah1:3–4; 2 Chronicles 20:3–10)
- When interceding for other people (Daniel 9:3)
- So that our spirits will readily be alive when God speaks (Acts 13:3–4)

How to Operate Biblical Fasting

One who is fasting needs to be very close to God, seeking His face in prayers and supplication for the duration of the fast. As already mentioned, there must be abstinence from food and drinks. After three days, drinking water is permissible and should be pure, warm, and adequate for hydration. When the person fasting needs to undertake heavy tasks or long distance journeys, other liquid drinks are advisable.

The duration of a fast should be a covenant between you and God and the purpose must be very clear; otherwise, the fast may be considered a waste of time, a hunger strike, or dieting. During periods of fasting, those who are married must be like those who are not—that is, abstain from sexual relationship (1 Corinthians 7:5).

There must be concerted prayers, adequate meditation on the Word and listening distinctly to the Holy Spirit for the duration of the fast. When the days are fulfilled, withdrawing from the fast should be done with all caution and discipline. You will need to exercise more self-control than when you were fasting so that your health is not impaired.

What Fasting Does to Your Health

Medical science tells us that fasting is excellent for good overall health-building because the digestive system should be given periodic rest.

The slogan is, "After you feast, you should fast." Explain what this means.

Conclusion

Apostle Paul declared that he was "fasting often" (2 Corinthians 11:27). Every believer should develop the lifestyle of fasting and praying on a regular basis. Jesus, David, Paul, and even the Pharisees fasted. Though a religious rite, fasting points to the deep commitment of any believer to the instructions of the Lord Jesus. When engaging in fasting and prayers, we must do so in a way that does not indicate to people that we are fasting (Matthew 6:16–18).

Memory Verse

> "And he said unto them this kind come forth by
> nothing, but by prayer and fasting" (Mark 9:29).

> "But those who wait on the Lord; shall renew their
> strength; they shall mount up with wings [soar] like
> eagles; they shall run and not be weary, they shall walk
> and not faint" (Isaiah 40:31).

Pull out your calendar and insert the day you will fast and pray, for yourself (spiritual revival), your family, your church, and your community.

Date
Purpose
Times of Prayers
Sign off on this (your name)

CHAPTER 14

Divine Healing

If you walk into a facility for the mentally disabled, you may be grateful for your sound mental orientation. If you learn of an abused woman who has been the victim of rape, molestation, or other diabolical use by men, you know that her psyche and emotional composition have been tampered with and that her psyche is not the way God created her. And you will believe that folks need divine healing. Whether it is physical ill health or emotional trauma, something has gone wrong in the world today. The original blueprint from God is no more. This is the reason Jesus declared:

> "The Spirit of the Lord is upon Me, because He has anointed Me to preach the gospel to the poor; He has sent Me to heal the brokenhearted, To proclaim liberty to the captives and recovery of sight to the blind, To set at liberty those who are oppressed; to proclaim the acceptable year of the Lord" (Luke 4:18–19 NKJV).

To properly administer medications to patients, doctors painstakingly go through series of tests and diagnoses to get to the root causes and then advise on the treatment path. In this chapter, we will look at the various forms of human malfunction and areas of need. Problem areas identified are as follows:

1. Physical ill-health
2. Psychological imbalance
3. Emotional trauma
4. Psychiatric disorder

The church has a responsibility to stem the tide of these cases by engaging in spiritual warfare and deliverance. Special sessions should be conducted to pray for these groups with dedication, compassion, and respect. This study is aimed at identifying issues while using the Word of God (the Bible) to diagnose them. Professional counselors may be involved, outside the spiritual mainstream. The real treatment involves praying and fasting over identified issues and conducting sessions of prayers of deliverance for folks in a respectful and orderly manner. Some of these combatant spiritual operations, however, cannot be done by any carnal Christian. Such a person must be on "fire" with the Holy Spirit and thoroughly be equipped to handle and be engaged in such spiritual operations.

God's knowledge of a human being can be likened to that of a manufacturer of an engine who must know all intricacies of the engine. He is the "subject matter expert" of man. As the chief architect of our nature and/or the manufacturer of all parts of our body, He knows what to do to any part that fails or falls out of harmony. He wants to heal us, to fix the broken pieces. We limit His power if we deny His healing ability. We need His healing touch, today more than ever, as witnessed by the apostles during Christ's ministry on earth.

"Beloved, I wish above all things that thou mayest prosper and be in health, even as thy soul prospereth" (3 John 1:2).

God is passionate about you! He wants you to prosper. He wants to heal you. In fact, He wants you to enjoy good health. He is also interested in your soul prospering.

1. Physical (body)—disease or infection of the anatomy and/or physiology of a human body

2. Psychological imbalance—unstable state of the psyche and self-esteem of the man

3. Emotional trauma—dismemberment of the fabrics of the inner man

4. Psychiatric disorder—alteration to the mental accent of a man

Please provide the information to the following table:

Man's Need	Today's Example	Strategies to Curb	Case-based example in Bible
Physical Body Healing			
Psychological Healing			
Emotional Healing			
Psychiatric Healing			
Prosperity from Above			

Psalms 139:14 says that we are fearfully and wonderfully made. This implies the perfect state of man at creation, after God finished creating man. He looked and considered the work He had just created and certified that "it was very good" (Genesis 1:31). So God created man perfectly, without ailment, disability, or disease. In His own perfect image, He created man (Genesis 1:27).

What are the sources of illness and disorders?

A few of the causes of the malfunctioning of man are outlined below, though not exhaustive. These are:

1. *Sin.* Man was tempted, sinned, and fell in the garden of Eden (Genesis 3:1–6), as God could no longer dwell in man because of

indwelling sin. The original and perfect state of man was lost. The presence of sin in man implies the presence of the Devil, and the presence of Satan means problems, woes, sickness, and affliction. The Devil is the author of all evil and there is nothing good in him (John 10:10a; Luke 13:14–16).

2. *Eating habits.* Malnutrition, overeating, smoking, and drugs alter the original configuration of the body and thus break it down (Proverbs 23:21). Overeating (gluttony) is likened to drunkenness. Your body is the temple of the living God.

3. *Curses and demonic attack* (Luke 13:16; Acts 13:9–11; Job 1:8–12:2, 7). Persons under the influence of some spiritual powers can curse another, resulting in a disorder. Being involving in occult practices or initiating into demon-orchestrated groups also invites mental derailment. When persons read books dedicated to Satan, there is a huge chance that the fellow will be affected by the spirit that empowers such writings. Other sources can be through overwork, sleeplessness, restlessness, anxiety, and worries (Proverbs 15:13; 17:22).

4. *Ancestral initiation.* If your forefathers were involved in certain demonic activities and even you, without knowing it, were initiated by blood, the tendency is that such initiation will still hold until you are delivered from that curse—for example, slave trade (buying or selling), demon worship, cult practice, or impulsive shedding of human blood (blood hunger) for whatever reason. Such blood cries for vengeance before the Father.

Healing in Jesus' Name

Our Lord Jesus Christ died and rose again to guarantee us perfect redemption. Part of the redemption package is our good health and power over sickness and disease (3 John 2; Isaiah 53:4–5; Matthew 8:17; 1 Peter 2:24; Luke 9:1–2). By redemption, we have been brought back to our former position, but because we lost that position to Satan, he is not going to let go easily—unless we send him packing by violence! (Matthew 11:12.

Here's what deliverance looks like:

> And when he came to his disciples, he saw a great multitude
> about them, and the scribes questioning with them. And
> straightway all the people, when they beheld him, were
> greatly amazed, and running to him saluted him. And
> he asked the scribes, What question ye with them? And
> one of the multitude answered and said, Master, I have
> brought unto thee my son, which hath a dumb spirit;
> And wheresoever he taketh him, he teareth him: and he
> foameth, and gnasheth with his teeth, and pineth away:
> and I spake to thy disciples that they should cast him out;
> and they could not. (Mark 9:14–18 KJV)

Jesus stepped in, and this fellow was delivered. Observe and learn deliverance the Jesus way:

> He answereth him, and saith, O faithless generation, how
> long shall I be with you? how long shall I suffer you? bring
> him unto me. And they brought him unto him: and when
> he saw him, straightway the spirit tare him; and he fell
> on the ground, and wallowed foaming. And he asked his
> father, How long is it ago since this came unto him? And
> he said, Of a child. And ofttimes it hath cast him into the
> fire, and into the waters, to destroy him: but if thou canst
> do anything, have compassion on us, and help us. Jesus
> said unto him, If thou canst believe, all things are possible
> to him that believeth. And straightway the father of the
> child cried out, and said with tears, Lord, I believe; help
> thou mine unbelief. When Jesus saw that the people came
> running together, he rebuked the foul spirit, saying unto
> him, Thou dumb and deaf spirit, I charge thee, come out
> of him, and enter no more into him. And the spirit cried,
> and rent him sore, and came out of him: and he was as
> one dead; insomuch that many said, He is dead. But Jesus
> took him by the hand, and lifted him up; and he arose.

And when he was come into the house, his disciples asked him privately, Why could not we cast him out? And he said unto them, This kind can come forth by nothing, but by prayer and fasting. (Mark 9:19–29 KJV)

You Too Can Conduct Deliverance for People…Only If …

When God calls, He empowers. His calling is without repentance, meaning that He does not withdraw His calling or gifting. Has God called you? Be patient, and find a place for training and mentorship. Learn at the feet of the Master, and be empowered by the Holy Spirit. The unction of the Spirit with wisdom and knowledge of the Word is all you need to go out and confront the evil. Until then, you may not want to go the battlefield, please.

"And John answered him, saying, Master, we saw one casting out devils in thy name, and he followeth not us: and we forbad him, because he followeth not us. But Jesus said, Forbid him not: for there is no man which shall do a miracle in my name, that can lightly speak evil of me. For he that is not against us is on our part" (Mark 9:38–40).

Identify from the above passage why the apostles were unable to cast out those demons.

Here's another scene, a pathetic one:

Then some of the itinerant Jewish exorcists undertook to invoke the name of the Lord Jesus over those who had evil spirits, saying, "I adjure you by the Jesus whom Paul proclaims." Seven sons of a Jewish high priest named Sceva were doing this. But the evil spirit answered them, "Jesus I know, and Paul I recognize, but who are you?" And the man in whom was the evil spirit leaped on them, mastered all four of them and overpowered them, so that they fled out of that house naked and wounded. And this became known to all the residents of Ephesus, both Jews and Greeks. And fear fell upon them all, and the name of the Lord Jesus was extolled. (Acts 19:13–17)

What drives men to seek financial gain with the gospel?

Receive Your Healing

Prayer by the sick person (James 5:13, 16b; John 14:11, 13–14; Philippians 2:9–11). Nothing hinders the Devil from trying you with a sickness but nothing stops you from rejecting his offer and dispatching it back to him with the speed of the Spirit of the Lord and in the name of Jesus. When you are ill, check if there is any sin in your life; if there is any, confess and repent of it, and thereafter, pray a prayer of healing for yourself. The result will amaze you if you do all things by faith (2 Kings 20:3–5).

By united or communal prayer of two or more Christians (Matthew 18:19; James 5:16a). This is why you need to belong to a church or fellowship that preaches the truth.

By laying hands on the sick person (Mark 16:18; Acts 9:17–18; 28:8). This must be done with caution. Ensure that you have consecrated your life and are living holy before laying hands on the sick (2 Corinthians 8:5; Romans 12:1, 6, 13). There could be transfer of spirits. Be careful!

Anointing the sick with oil and prayer of faith by elders (James 5:14–15). In certain quarters, people engage in no scriptural ceremonies like ritual washing, burning candles, holy water, or putting on a cross. These are unnecessary encumbrances that plague Christian faith. The Bible says the prayer of faith and nothing else (Matthew 5:25–29). Do not import foreign ideology into the church of God.

By divine authority and power Persons or clergy of higher spiritual authority can break curses and set a captive free. They do this in the name of Jesus Christ.

Just before Israel marched across the Jordan River to begin their conquest of Canaan, they stopped in Moab to camp. Balak, the king of Moab, was worried that they would go to war against him, so he summoned a pagan prophet named Balaam, the son of Beor, to curse Israel so Moab would not be conquered. Balaam had a reputation for being a successful magician of sorts. The people he blessed were blessed, and those he cursed were cursed (Numbers 22:6). The Lord told Balaam not to go to Balak because Israel was blessed. But Balaam was going to go to Balak anyway, because he was greedy (2 Peter 2:15). So the Lord changed His mind and told him he could go but only if he said what God told him to say. Even if someone claims to have spiritual authority over you, the Lord can overturn the curse placed by that person (Numbers 22–24; 31:1–17).

Can a Christian be possessed by a demon? Hold this discussion based on these Scriptures: Mark 1:23–24; Luke 4:33–36; Acts 16:16–18.

How to Keep Your Healing and Remain Healthy

You must be born again (John 3:3; 16:36). Note that healing is the children's bread (Mark 7:24–27).

After salvation, you must live in obedience. Do not engage in sinful acts anymore (Deuteronomy 7:12, 15; Isaiah 1:18–20; John 5:14; James 4:7).

Worship God continually in spirit and in truth (John 4:24)

Fast and pray often (Isaiah 58:6, 8).

When Satan tries you with illness, confess what the Word of God says about your healing and claim the promises. Confess strength always; do not confess weakness (1 Corinthians 3:16–17; Joel 3:10).

Conclusion

Divine healing operates in the realm of dominion. God wants to take you there. To rely on medication for every illness is not sinful but indicates you are still far from where God wants you to be. Develop a strong faith against sickness, based on the Word of God, and you will find yourself walking in the realm of dominion.

Memory Verse

> "Who his own self bare our sins in his own body on
> the tree, that we, being dead to sins should live unto
> righteousness: by whose stripes ye were healed" (1 Peter
> 2:24).

Notes

CHAPTER 15

Grace and Truth

Here's Grace ...

Suppose Osama bin Laden and all the people who masterminded the 9/11 attack on the World Trade Center had been in the United States before September 2011, and there was rumor that foreign faces were seen around the Capitol and Pentagon.

Suddenly, the terrorists hit. New York firefighters gave their lives trying to rescue people trapped in the World Trade Center. Suppose the only ones trapped were the terrorists who caused the explosion. Suppose it was Osama bin Laden who was stuck in that building, and he was known to have masterminded the crime. Make it more personal: imagine a soldier who lost his wife and child in the World Trade Center because bin Laden ordered those suicide bombings. Imagine him carrying bin Laden out of the smoke and dust, giving him water, and nursing him back to health. Unthinkable? Isn't it? That's getting closer to grace.

Defining Truth

Truth is a validated and proven fact of life. It has no gray area of interpretation but stands out with a perfect conclusion of an issue, statement or analysis in any given environment or within a group. Truth is a constant, and constants do not change. They are absolutes, never shifting from their positions. Truth is a personality that has potential to grow and blossom. Truth is rooted in the eternal God who is all powerful and unchangeable. Therefore, His promises cannot fail.

Jesus prayed, "Sanctify them by the truth; Your word is Truth" (John 17:17). Not only can we depend on Scripture, but we can be transformed and sanctified by it.

What Truth Is Not

1. Truth does not change with changing circumstances, though it is an agent of change.
2. Truth is not a moral guide. Jesus declared, "I am the way, the truth and the life; no man comes to the Father but by Me" (John 14:6). He did not say He would show the truth or teach the truth or model the truth. He is the truth. He is truth personified. He is the source of all truth, the embodiment of truth and therefore, the reference point for evaluating all truth claims.
3. Truth is not a suggestion to live right or do some spectacular things.
4. Truth does not advertise itself but stays docile and calm, affecting its hearers.
5. Truth is not an idea or a localized or regionalized code of behavior; it outlives the carrier.
6. Name other things that truth is not:

7. Truth is seen as a vapor that spreads, never contained or restricted. Share your insights into the nature and constitution of this vapor.

What Truth Is

1. Truth is life.
2. Truth changes lives and sanctifies the heart

3. Truth, when used to describe people, can show integrity of thoughts, speech, or actions. Truth is the bedrock of human relationships (Exodus 20:16).
4. Truth is reality. It's the way things really are. In over 50 percent of Paul's writings in John, the New Testament uses "truth" (*aletheia* in Greek, meaning "disclosure").
5. To know the truth is to see accurately. To believe what is not true is to be blind. God has written His truth on human hearts, in the conscience (Romans 2:15). When the world hears truth, if spoken graciously, many are drawn to it by the moral vacuum they feel. The heart longs for truth; even the heart that rejects it.
6. The Holy Spirit leads men into truth (John 16:13). Christ's disciples know the truth (John 8:32), they do the truth (John 3:21), and they abide in the truth (John 8:44). We are commanded to know the truth (1 Timothy 4:3), handle the truth accurately (2 Timothy 2:25), and avoid doctrinal untruths (2 Timothy 2:18). The "belt of truth" holds together our spiritual armor (Ephesians 6:14).
7. Jesus is the truth and the life.

Lies the Devil Is Passing On in Our Age and Churches

1. "Open theology," which contends that God doesn't know what future choices people will make
2. Waning belief in an eternal punishment or human depravity. It is proposed that hell fire is what you experience on earth, whatever your situation dictates; belief that a good God cannot put people in hell, so there is no hell.
3. Sexual behavior is acceptable, even outside of marriage. "We are bed mates; nothing is wrong with it."
4. Heterosexuals and homosexuals are the same. Lesbians and gays should be given equal opportunity to lead the church. It is politically acceptable. (Permit me to say, "Even my dog would oppose that and groan at the church.")
5. The Scripture is *not* the authoritative source for living. "I will not allow God's Word to persuade me to believe what I do not

like; what is contrary to what I have always believed and want to believe." The question should be asked, "Do I believe it's correct when it offends me?"

6. Open-ended theology: a "you can have it all" worldview is a hodgepodge of biblical truth, undefined spirituality, and psychology, with twelve-step recovery and self-affirmations. The open-ended theology is a church-free build-it-yourself spirituality that never condemns. It speaks often of a higher power—sometimes God, sometimes Jesus.

7. Generic spirituality: all roads lead to heaven. Karma. Mohammed. Reincarnation. Buddhism. Hinduism. New Age. Angel-guided living. It's a "Have it your way" designer religion made to order for a post-Christian culture. "Now the Bereans were of more noble character than the Thessalonians, for they received the message with great eagerness and examined the Scriptures every day to see if what Paul said was true" (Acts 17:11).

8. Amorphous, shape-shifting faith that slides to the contours of individual preferences. This nurtures our tendency to self-edification, in which we strive to be our own gods, setting our own standards, and controlling our own mini-universes. "Do it my way" kind of thing.

9. Hydra-headed path to God, which suggests that "the biggest mistakes humans make is to believe there is only one way." And adds that there are many diverse paths leading to what you call God. In the meantime, God says, "Neither is there any other name under heaven given among men whereby we must be saved" (Acts 4:12). Jesus remains the hub and center of all creation and path to God. There is no alternative path to seeking God.

10. "Truth is whatever you sincerely believe is true." "There's no such thing as truth"—is this a true statement? If so, then the statement proves itself wrong. (Why does anyone go to college to learn truth from professors who believe there is no truth?) Jesus Christ is the truth and the life.

11. Moral relativism: church pews filled with all-inclusive doctrinal backlashes, "come as you are; remain the way you came"; "gather the tithes and offerings for our next project." This has no spiritual

content toward heaven or toward God. Moral relativism has no underlying substance to hold its structure or contend for what it believes is right. Relativism floats on the whims of what is socially and all-inclusively prevailing. It has no core values.

12. Freedom to live in sin because we are "saved by grace, do anything under grace (including living in sin), and still are on our way to heaven." A woman preacher (a televangelist) walked away from her marriage without biblical grounds because, in her words, "The Holy Spirit gave me peace about it." She also said, "It is turning out for the glory of God, and the ministry is moving forward." She is still preaching and raising followers in the church, claiming the spiritual high ground. She said, "I've never been so close to God." There is a looming "Ichabod" on the wall!

"As the reservoir empties itself into the pipes, so hath Christ emptied out His grace into His people. He stands like a fountain, always flowing, to supply the empty pitchers and the thirsty lips which draw near to it. Grace, whether it is working to pardon, to cleanse, to preserve, is ever to be had from Him freely and without price."

—Charles Spurgeon

"Like the liberals before us, evangelicals use the Bible's words but give them new meaning, pouring bad secular content into spiritual terminology; differently, of course, we live in a therapeutic age now. So evangelicals have recast their theology in psychiatric terms."

—James Boice

"People once looked to Scripture for grace and truth. Now, for truth, they look to science, education, and media. For grace, they look to psychology, recovery groups, and social repair programs."

Understanding addictions involves two warring alternatives—the sin model and the disease model. Truth advocates embrace the sin model, which is solved by repentance and reformation. Grace advocates follow the disease model, which is solved by understanding and compassion. So what is the answer—grace or truth? Neither of the two can stand alone. Both truth and grace go together; we obtain a balanced score card when we integrate both grace and truth. (Excerpted from *The Grace and Truth Paradox: Teaching* by Randy Alcorn of Eternity Perspective Ministries.)

According to 1 Timothy 4:1–11 and 2 Timothy 3:1–9, Paul advised Timothy to beware of false teachers. Mention some of the prevailing errors discussed in the two passages:

What is apostasy?

In your own opinion, what can your church do to stop the advancement of doctrines and teachings that defy the Godhead and all that Christ, the church, and the Holy Spirit stand for?

Assurance of Salvation

When you buy a car, the Department of Motor Vehicles' license office insists that you insure your car against incidental damage or collision. The same goes with a purchase of your home. Your home insurance is a condition to the purchase you make. The government wants to insure these assets in the event the unexpected happens. An insurance company underwrites accruable expenses. Have you ever asked this question: What if the insurance company goes under water? Who pays? Who comes to the rescue? Banks and insurance companies are usually insured under a "big brother." These are NDIC or reinsurance companies; an example is American International Group, Inc. (AIG). AIG is an American multinational insurance corporation with more than 88 million customers in 130 countries. AIG companies employ over 64,000 people in ninety countries. The company operates through three core businesses: AIG Property Casualty, AIG Life and Retirement, and United Guaranty

Corporation (UGC). AIG Property Casualty provides insurance products for commercial, institutional, and individual customers. AIG Life and Retirement provides life insurance and retirement services in the United States, and UGC focus on mortgage guaranty insurance and mortgage insurance. AIG also focuses on global capital markets operations, direct investment, and retained interests. Now you understand why the Fed swiftly bailed the AIG when it threatened to pull the plug on the financial market. As AIG provides cover to the insurance companies, insurance companies provide the same cover to the man on the street. The assurance (peace of mind) the consumer has is resting on the fact that should the worst happen, AIG or NDIC will come to the rescue.

In our faith, our walk with the Lord, and the journey of life, while we have leverages with meal tickets, education, or whatever lends to success in life, our faith rests on the bottom line. The assurance we have is in the fact that after all things are completed, we have this confidence that Jesus Christ will definitely bail us out of the mire, just because we have faith in Him. That the promise of the Father "to give us the kingdom" is an established line of truth and a promissory note that we can cash any time because, by the Holy Ghost, it has been engraved in our hearts forever and affirmed by the word of God.

At conversion, God made an exchange. He removed the heart of stone and replaced it with the heart of flesh. We became born again and our names were written in the Book of Life. The Holy Spirit came in and took charge, and we were changed. The presence of the Holy Spirit is the receipt for the transaction, and the peace oozing out of such transformed lives is proof that there is an occupant in the house that God just acquired. This is assurance of salvation.

Question:
How can I have assurance of my salvation?
1 John 5:11–13; John 1:12; Romans 10:9; John 10:28–29

If we confess our sins, He is faithful and just to forgive us our sins and to cleanse us from all unrighteousness. What, then, can separate us from the love of God, which is in Christ Jesus?

Restitution

Restitution is paying back what is owed to the original owner. It is a confession that is made for wrongful acts or impersonations that deprived someone of his rights or privileges. In political quarters, they call it reparation—"the making of amends for a wrong one has done, by paying money to or otherwise helping those who have been wronged; it is the action of repairing something." Reparation money is paid to a country or group that loses a war because of the damage, injury, and/or deaths incurred. The paying country caused the receiving country hardship or pain.

What is restitution, and how do we provide it? (Leviticus. 6:1–7; Luke 19:8). Restitution involves restoring to the owner all things taken by falsehood, confessing all lies told, declaring to all the people who were deceived, and painting the tacit picture of things. (Proverbs 6:30–31; 28:13; Acts 24:16; Ezekiel 33:14–16; 2 Samuel 12:1–6; Philippians 1:10; Leviticus 6:2–5). It is being willing to let the Lord expose and then heal painful areas of our past.

God commands that restitution be made. Restitution leaves behind an indelible testimony with the one to whom restitution is made; which "when an unbeliever is involved becomes a means of preaching the gospel of Jesus Christ." When restitution is made to unsaved ones, undoing wrongs done against an organization, or to those that affect marriage relationships, restitution may require much prayer and counseling from men of God.

> **"The true test of one's faith is activity at the altar of renunciation, reconciliation, and confession of wrongs done against people, which sometimes can lead to a loss of acquired gains prior to conversion"**

Examples of Restitution
Zacchaeus and Onesimus

> And Jesus entered and passed through Jericho. And, behold, there was a man named Zacchaeus, which was

the chief among the publicans, and he was rich. And he sought to see Jesus who he was; and could not for the press, because he was little of stature. And he ran before, and climbed up into a sycamore tree to see him: for he was to pass that way. And when Jesus came to the place, he looked up, and saw him, and said unto him, Zacchaeus, make haste, and come down; for today I must abide at thy house. And he made haste, and came down, and received him joyfully. And when they saw it, they all murmured, saying that he was gone to be guest with a man that is a sinner. And Zacchaeus stood, and said unto the Lord: "Behold, Lord, the half of my goods I give to the poor; and if I have taken anything from any man by false accusation, I restore him fourfold." And Jesus said unto him, "This day is salvation come to this house, forsomuch as he also is a son of Abraham. For the Son of man is come to seek and to save that which was lost." (Luke 19:1–10)

Paul's Plea for Onesimus; He Writes Philemon

I appeal to you for my son Onesimus who became my son while I was in chains. Formerly he was useless to you, but now he has become useful both to you and to me. I am sending him—who is my very heart; back to you ... If he has done you any wrong or owes you anything, charge it to me. I, Paul, am writing this with my own hand. I will pay it back—not to mention that you owe me your very self. I do wish, brother, that I may have some benefit from you in the Lord; refresh my heart in Christ. (Philemon 1:10–12, 18–20)

Matthew was a tax collector, one who defrauded people of their money by collecting more than the government's required amount. He was notorious for that. Onesimus was a slave boy to Philemon and had stolen from his master. *Easton's Bible Dictionary* describes him as "useful." Useful—a slave who, after robbing his master Philemon at Colosse, fled to Rome, where he was converted by the apostle Paul sent him back to his master with the letter that bears his name. In it, he begs Philemon to receive his slave as a "faithful and beloved brother." Paul offered to repay Philemon anything his slave had taken and to bear the wrong he had done. He was accompanied on his return by Tychicus, the bearer of the epistle to the Colossians (Philemon 1:6, 18).

The story of this fugitive Colossian slave is a remarkable evidence of the freedom of access to the prisoner that was granted to all, and it is a beautiful illustration of the character of Paul and the transfiguring power and righteous principles of the gospel. It further reinstates that nothing received or obtained in pretense or falsehood should ever be taken and owned after conversion. Since Onesimus had squandered the money belonging to his master, Philemon; Paul owned up to the repayment.

In your own words, what is restitution? (Leviticus 6:1–7; Luke 19:8)

How do we make restitution?

Restitution involves making amends and holding a good testimony before God and man (Proverbs 6: 30–31; 28:13; Acts 24:16; Ezekiel 33:14–16; 2 Samuel 12:1–6; Philemon 1:10; Leviticus 6:2–5). What if the object of restitution touches on marriage fidelity? How do you handle that?

Zacchaeus said, "I will restore fourfold ..." What does that tell us about Zacchaeus' conversion?

Where do you think grace, mercy, and truth meet regarding restoring and maintaining good testimonies before God and man? Be practical!

In ministry, especially when the "go, go" urge is imminent and peers are asking you to start fellowship or a church (even when you are still being mentored), you scheme over your mentor or "snatch" the members of an existing church. What type of restitution is expected in this situation, if the preacher must show signs of genuine conversion?

Identify areas or items that are most difficult to restore; and please state why

Healing begins with the ability to let go and accept responsibility and consequences for our past actions, allowing the Lord to expose our raw, old, Adam-like nature and nail them to the cross. This is a pain most Christians would not want to go through. God commands that restitution be made. Restitution leaves behind an indelible testimony with the one to whom restitution is made, which, when an unbeliever is involved, becomes a means of preaching the gospel of Jesus Christ. Restitution involving unsaved ones, or undoing wrongs done against organizations or those that affect marriage relationships requires prayers, counseling, and diving into the ultimate purpose of the restitution in question. Restitutions are made to foster a healthier relationship, develop a deeper commitment with God, and enrich and edify the church of Christ to God's glory. It is not aimed at exterminating the faith of the believer or putting a curse on the actor of restitution; instead, the person should be edified to go the long haul with God and man in the Christian experience.

CHAPTER 16

Moral Issues

She had an angelic face and a lovely figure, but Angel was more to her name than words could describe. Beautiful, cute, charming, and dangerously inviting—these descriptions could not capture her. At the Miss World beauty pageant, Angel won first place over her competitors. She was a complete package of beauty and intelligence, but she lacked one thing.

As the years went on, the smooth flesh and muscles of her face yielded to weak veins; age muted her beauty, as the sunset had begun. The presence of age was not negotiable; it was a necessity that must be. Angel's life has been a public spectacle; a wealthy lady who was able to control men of any status imaginable.

The cosmetic infusions and plastic surgeries over the years suddenly showed up disguised as cancer. Too late to gather her mind to focus on her Maker, she was ebbing out like a vapor. Her body had been used to society's acclaim and ovation; her psyche had been plundered, and the spirit was sick toward God. Her life had become a tale told by an idiot; full of sound and fury.

God's standard does not change with time, and His views have not shifted because of multitudes engaged in sinful behaviors. If sinners entice you, do not consent to their luring invitations; do not follow the multitudes to commit sin. Keep yourself pure and abstain from the sin of adultery and fornication.

What is adultery?

Does it belong to the Old Testament period? (Exodus 20:14; 1 Corinthians 6:9–10).

Adultery involves breaking solemn marriage vows and defiling the conjugal bed (1 Corinthians 6:15–16; Hebrews 13:4).

What is fornication?

Is virginity outdated?

1 Corinthians 6:13; 18a Ephesians 5:3; Romans 12:2
Although fornication is a common practice among the young and teens, that does not make it acceptable to God. Brothers and sisters, keep yourselves pure.
What does sexual perversion mean?

Leviticus 18:22–23; Romans 1:26–27. Remember Sodom and Gomorrah.
Flirting is showing affection to the opposite sex, with intentions of or acting toward seducing or taking to bed. Love is too serious for play-acting. Paul warned Timothy in 1 Timothy 5:2, Do not send out wrong signals (Romans 14:16; Ephesians 4:27). Be wise; ensure you keep a safe distance from a member of the opposite gender if you are not convinced you are meant for each other. The closer you are, the more your hormones

get aroused. The more you get aroused, the more likely there will be the tendency to express yourself in sexual immorality.

Can a man take coals of fire into his garment and not be burned?

Read Proverbs 4 and 5. What do you see?

Dangers of Sexual Sin

1. God regards it as a waste resource (Proverbs 29:3).
2. As a vow-breaker, one is under a curse (Isaiah 54:5; Malachi 2:14).
3. It desecrates the blood-purchased property of Jesus and hence attracts destruction (1 Corinthians 6:19–20).
4. It is a sin against one's body (1 Corinthians 6:18).
5. It opens an access for the Devil's attack (Ecclesiastics 10:8b).

The world may outwardly laugh at you yet inwardly admire Christians who have the courage to stand up to their moral chastity.

Gays and Lesbians

What is wrong with homosexuality? (Romans 1:18–28)

When Lot went off course from Abraham to seek the green pastures and sensual desires of his heart, it was obvious that he had many of this world's goods, but his soul was sold out to the pleasures of sin. He dwelt in the ally side of Sodom and got mixed with the lifestyle of Gomorrah. He had no moral authority to rebuke sin. When God wanted to destroy the city, Abraham pleaded to see if God was willing to spare it because Lot was supposed to be a representative of heaven and its kingdom.

Check out the conversation between the Lord and Abraham: "Then the men turned away from there and went toward Sodom but Abraham still stood before the Lord; and Abraham came near and said; 'Would you also destroy the righteous with the wicked? Suppose there were fifty righteous within the city would you also destroy the place and not spare it for the fifty righteous that were in it?'" (Genesis 18:22–33).

The conversation went on until Abraham was stuck at ten righteous people, and that, God did not find. The driver of the sins of Sodom and Gomorrah was homosexuality. Men mating men; women mating women—this is a serious abomination before God, because in the beginning, God made them male and female. God was looking for only ten souls to spare the land. Had Lot had the testimony of Abraham, maybe God would have spared Sodom and Gomorrah. God said concerning Abraham:

"For I have known him so that he may command his children and his household after him, that they keep the way of the Lord, to do righteousness and justice; that the Lord will bring to Abraham what he had spoken to him" (Genesis 18:19). He would engaged in the pursuit of righteousness in the land. At least his converts would be his two sons-in-law and their fathers and mother, making a total of six. Add that to Lot, his wife, and two daughters, and you have a total of ten people saved and righteous. But that did not happen; instead, the Lord said, "Because the outcry against Sodom and Gomorrah is great and because their sin is very grave, I will go down now and see whether they have done altogether according to the outcry against it that has come to me and if not, I will know" (Genesis 18:20–21).

Why was it that Lot, his wife, and two daughters could not convert the people? To live as gays and lesbians is a serious abomination before God; indeed, it grieves His heart. For this reason, God allows him to have his way. In Romans 1:18, God declares that the wrath of God is revealed from heaven against all ungodliness and unrighteousness of men who suppress the truth in unrighteousness.

"Likewise also the men, leaving the natural use of women, burned in their lust for one another, men with men committing what is shameful and receiving in themselves the penalty of their error which was due. and even as they did not like to retain God in their knowledge, God gave them over to a debased (reprobate) mind, to do the things which are not fitting" (Romans 1:27–28).

What is the problem with a man marrying a man or a woman taking a woman as a wife?

Discuss how all these began and share any example of such happening in the animal kingdom.

How do we treat such people in the church of God?

Those struggling with homosexuality are humans. Like people struggling with other sins, they need the light; they need our prayers. The victims are helpless and are seeking a savior. We can be the savior they seek. As we reach out to them, we must be careful to love them and pray that the power that holds such people be broken so that men may truly experience the power of the risen Christ.

Courtship

First, let's establish that God did not lay some preapproval events before marriage. If courtship is a pre-marriage setting, a taste of what is to come, to see if it will work out well, then it is not of God, because the whole process is not orchestrated by faith. Anything done outside of faith is sin. In our day, when energy is exerted toward fighting the insurgent homosexual sin, it seems the church has withdrawn from the fight against sexual sin by the married and the unmarried. Christian parents arrange or encourage a night out for boys and girls … and we know nothing good happens at midnight among boys and girls.

But if courtship is a period of discovering and understanding each other after the fact, then it is to be encouraged and must be done in righteousness and purity of all purpose and intention. When there is consent, an agreement, or an expressed will to marry him or her, then the show begins. Sometimes, knowledge of the person requires the wisdom of the pastor or elders in your community to properly hash things out for the young people. Before courting, let someone (leader, mentor, pastor) guide you.

In whom would you confide to share your story of who you want to marry?

According to Genesis 24:1–4 and 36:18 (compare with Genesis 28:6–9), differentiate between the choices of Isaac, Jacob, and Esau.

Where do you have a date? Suggest the right venues.

What is wrong with the other locations?

List the most important things for discussion during the time of discovery and getting to know each other.
1.
2.
3.
4.
5.

As a young man or woman, marriage is an excitement, you seek to be involved. What are the expectations?

Courtship provides opportunities to share details about the following cases in your life:

1. Your roots
2. Financial situations
3. DNA and blood groups (genotypes)
4. Family tree/history
5. Your commitment to extended family
6. Plan for kids
7. Education and other training classes
8. Health issues
9. Your strong points
10. Your weaknesses
11. Your career
12. The call of God in your life
13. Where you want to live and retire (house and home)
14. Any other thing(s) important to you
15. Execution strategies for above listed items

In the interest of companionship and mutual relationship, two people who agree to marry should base their relationship on common beliefs and same lifestyles. What is the place of 2 Corinthians 6:12–14?

What do you understand to be "unequally yoked together"?

Before you agree to a date, how do you know God is leading you to the man or woman who is showing an interest in you? Tell how you know God's will in other areas of your life.

Is it right for a girl or woman to ask a boy or man to marry her?

Why?

At eighteen, a boy or girl is assumed to be an adult in most advanced countries. What is the right age for marriage, and what are the consequences of early or immature marriage?

When is a man or woman considered mature enough to date and then marry?

Maturity is a function of the following. Please explain how these affect your choice and timing in marriage:
1. Age or physiological growth
2. Financial stability
3. Spiritual growth
4. Emotional stability
5. Psychological growth

What is the driver (main object of decision) in your choice of the person you are dating? Why?

Beauty
Immigration papers
Profession
Ethnicity or tribal extraction
Wealth
Spirituality
Wisdom
Mention others

Any relationship that is established on righteousness and open disclosure of a secret lifestyle forms a good foundation. Focusing on the right thing will stand in the days of adversity. When we allow God to form the foundation of our relationships (by yielding to the finished work of Christ, studying and obeying the Word of God daily, and having a deep communication with Him, not neglecting worshipping with other believers), then the relationships can claim to have formed a good foundation. Until then, our expectations or drivers have no substance in them and can, at any day or time, be gone or diminished. If courtship is based on any or all the above list of drivers without the right thing, then you may experience a setback when such driver is gone.

During a date, boys and girls usually tell one another the good, sweet stories about themselves. A courtship that is aimed at marriage presupposes that reality will soon be on display, when "the man and the woman will both be naked before each other." The secret things are exposed, and reality stares at each one's face. It is therefore wholesome to engage the services of a Christian counselor, the pastor or an elder of the church, or a community leader to provide counsel to people during courtship. It is in the counseling room that facts and truths about marriage are discussed and understood, where we discover the details of marriage.

Courting and then marrying are necessary phases in life. How do you navigate the waters? Who is your teacher (counselor), and where would you want to learn the art and processes of marriage?

Mentor or teacher

Where to learn (church, fellowship, etc)

Who signs off on this?

What is the Bible-approved process of getting engaged or asking for someone's hand in marriage, as a believer in Jesus Christ?

Study the following passages: 1 Samuel 16:7; Genesis 24:1–4; Thessalonians 4:1–7; Proverbs 9:17–18; Hebrews 13:4. Summarize lessons learned and actionable points you have decided to undertake in your courtship. List them here:

Courtship: Petting, romance, and sex are abominations before God during courtship. Ensure that you and your intended spouse have a common understanding of the doctrines of the Bible.

Keep yourselves pure!

CHAPTER 17

Money Matters

Exodus 35:5–19, 30–35; 36:6–7; Acts 6:1–7

"The evils that men do live in money, exacerbated by pride, deeply rooted in the orgy, running quest to fill an empty lust"

In prehistoric times, business was done by trade and barter, in which the one who had a commodity brought something to exchange for something that another person had. Life was good and easy. Then came the era of cowries—shells used as currency. Cowries became the means of exchange. The seas and oceans somehow became the currency-minting house. I believe the church thrived and had little or nothing to worry about. Whether it was an organized church or the church in homes and villages, at least communal living and caring for the other folks out there was important to their daily routines. People's tastes and desires had not gone beyond their means; men lived according to the provisioning of Mother Nature, according to the yield from their farms. There were no high-tech tablets, iPhones, iPads, or latest sporty, luxury cars, and all the good stuff that drives our quest to buy and be happy today.

Then, life was pristine, adequate, and concise. Man was contained by his wants, contrary to today's unfettered drive to possess his needs. Today, man is occupied with satisfying the ego and sensual desires of his flesh.

These are the reasons why we, in part, engage our energies in the wrong use of money.

Handling Money: How Do You Fare?

Consider these characters and share what you've learned from their ways of handling or using money:
1. Ananias and Sapphire (Acts 5)
2. Simon the sorcerer (Acts 8:9-20)
3. Judas Iscariot (John 13:21; 26-30
4. Gehazi, servant of Elijah (2 Kings 5:20–27)
5. Priest at the Temple (Nehemiah 7:63-65; 13:3-10)

The Bible does not condemn money per se but gives some safe guidelines on the attitude of the Christian toward money. Money, seen and used as a tool toward meeting needs, would benefit many a Christian. The love of money has caused many sorrows in homes and churches, the reason for these nuggets:

Do not love money (1Timothy 6:6–10). The remedy is contentment with what God provides.

Do not be too preoccupied with searching for money at the expense of God (Matthew 6:33).

Do not hoard it up (Matthew 6:19; 1 Timothy 6:17). Your financial strength has no bearing in heaven or hell. This is a note of caution (Revelations 3:1-3; 17-19).

Do not worship money (Matthew 6:24; Proverbs 11:28). Money should not be your god. No idolater shall inherit the kingdom of God.

Do not live in debt as a way of life. Be content with your earnings (1Timothy 6:6). The only Bible-recommended debt is love (Romans 13:8).

Remember, you have been bought with a price (1 Corinthians 6:20). Your money belongs to your Master; you are only a custodian (1 Corinthians 4:2–7; Deuteronomy 8:18).

Do not put your trust in your money (1 Timothy 6:17; Psalms 62:10b).

Do not be involved in extortion, bribery, or corruption (Isaiah 33:15).

Biblical Principles of Giving

On what basis does your giving derive its lifeline?

Why must someone give away his hard-earned dollars to charity or a church

Love, as a principles ought to form the basis on why you should give.

> *"For God so loved the world that He gave His*
> *only begotten Son ..." (John 3:16)*

We give because God showed us an example, being our Father. We appreciate the Ultimate Giver by giving to His cause and those who cannot help themselves (Deuteronomy 8:18). Giving also allows us demonstrate love we received from the Father; with an opportunity to sow God's eternal truth in someone's life (Proverbs 14:21). It is an expression of the true conversion we have received. We give in order to avoid the trap of stinginess (Proverbs 11:25–26; 2 Corinthians 9:6). We also give to the church for the gospel work; to keep the sanctuary (bills to pay) and to take care of the clergy and all the employees of the church or fellowship group.

What do you give?

Money: How much do you think your salvation and health are worth?

Skills: When last did you apply your skill set to your local church or fellowship as a way of volunteer service?

Write down what you will do in your church or fellowship this month.

Time: (Romans 12:11–12). The complaint about lack of time to execute certain projects is pretending to be ignorant or naive about the true state of things. Time is a constant, measurable resource that should not be wasted. For example, to receive a message from God involves the use of time, and to get a job completed in your community requires time. So to refrain from doing a task for the kingdom's purpose does not mean there was no time. You simply do not want to do such tasks, maybe for many reasons. Thus, the phrase "I don't have time" should be revised to "I don't have time for you."

How do you allocate time for the work in your fellowship with your official work?

How do you invest your time in the ministry?

Prayers: (Luke 2:36–38; Philippians 1:3–11; Daniel 9)

The gift of prayer is a rare blessing. Many in the church do not fully understand its importance and thus the place, power, and practice have suffered a setback. Prayer, seen as a commitment and a lifestyle, especially the intercessory type, is aligned with the ministry work and the processes that yield to the overall objective of the mandate from God.

Ministry begs for sustenance (with prayers) by those who choose to labor behind the scene, unnoticed, yet providing potency and a lifeline to the work of the kingdom. Those who give themselves to prayers and support are seldom seen. These are the great generals of the faith, the unseen performers. Thus, the gift of prayer and the need in the church are synonymous with God's approval and mandates to spread the gospel to everyone.

Prayer—real prayer—comes from a red-hot passion to deliver a message and to partner with God in search of an open heaven for the people. "And I sought for a man who will stand in the gap [between God and man] and there was none" (Ezekiel 22:30). That was God's query as men of prayer have taken to their personal schemes and projects, leaving behind serious spiritual occupation in the hands of novices. Give the gift of prayer for the church.

Giving Materials Substance
Exodus 35:4–35

"Do not store up for yourselves treasures on earth, where moths and vermin destroy, and where thieves break in and steal; But store up for yourselves treasures in heaven, where moths and vermin do not destroy, and where thieves do not break in and steal. For where your treasure is, there your heart will be also" (Matthew 6:19–21 NIV).

To whom do you give?
1. To the church or organization to do God's work—missions, church planting (1 Corinthian 8–9; Acts 13:5)
2. Spiritual leaders—Levites, Priests, Ministers (1 Corinthians 9:1-19)
3. Less privileged (Proverbs 19:17)

4. Building the sanctuary (Exodus 28, 35, 36)
5. Community program (Acts 4:32–37)

How do you give?
1. Freely and cheerfully. It attracts God's attention and blessings (Proverbs 11:24; 2 Corinthians 9:7).
2. In proportion to your earnings and harvest of your farms (Acts 11:29; 2 Corinthians 8:1–3; Mark 12:41–44).
3. Give without publicity (Matthew 6:1–4).

When giving is tied to an expectation of a tax refund from the IRS, how does that affect our obedience to the mandate to give freely without the person next door being aware of it? Discuss this with practical balance.

Note: Wealth made through illegal or corrupt means and given for God's cause cannot pacify God's anger against a sinner (Psalms 26:9–10; 1 Corinthians 6:9–10). You cannot buy a good relationship with God.

Tithes in the Church

A tithe is 10 percent of your total or gross income. It belongs to God (Malachi 3:8–12; Leviticus 27:30). When you pay a tithe, it is *not* a sacrifice but an act of returning to God what He has given you, which belongs to Him. It is not optional (Matthew 12:1; Mark 2:23; Luke 6:1; Malachi 3:10).

"At that time Jesus went through the grain fields on the Sabbath. His disciples were hungry and began to pick some heads of grain and eat them" (Matthew 12:1).

"When you are harvesting in your field and you overlook a sheaf, do not go back to get it. Leave it for the foreigner, the fatherless and the widow, so that the LORD your God may bless you in all the work of your hands" (Deuteronomy 24:19).

"And Ruth the Moabite said to Naomi, 'Let me go to the fields and pick up the leftover grain behind anyone in whose eyes I find favor.' Naomi said to her, 'Go ahead, my daughter.' … As she got up to glean, Boaz gave orders to his men, 'Let her gather among the sheaves and don't reprimand her'" (Ruth 2:2, 15 NIV).

"On this day you shall make a proclamation as well; you are to have a holy convocation. You shall do no laborious work. It is to be a perpetual statute in all your dwelling places throughout your generations. 'When you reap the harvest of your land, moreover, you shall not reap to the very corners of your field nor gather the gleaning of your harvest; you are to leave them for the needy and the alien. I am the LORD your God'" (Leviticus 23:21–22).

Why pay tithes?

When we earn a salary, the government takes 10–30 percent of that money as income tax. The more you earn, the more is taken out of your paycheck. Government uses taxes to fix roads and for schools, public property, the military, police and fire fighters and for all the things we enjoy in our community. We take the remainder of our salary to the store to buy household needs, and we are taxed again. The system may run freely for the good of all. The same goes with the church. Paying tithes and giving generally for the cause of God's work on earth is an exemplification of the relationship one has with the Father.

In the United States, visitors do not pay taxes because they are not in the system. They are not allowed to be compensated for whatever work they do because they are visitors; they are aliens. Citizens pay taxes and have access to resources provided by the state and federal governments.

The same goes with the kingdom of God and His church. Kingdom citizens pay their tithes. They give to the system to sustain it and keep it running. In fact, paying tithes is the minimum that is expected of a kingdom citizen by way of commitment and involvement. It is a baseline, a foundation to all giving and is therefore not negotiable.

Why is a tithe the minimum amount expected?

Check out these Scriptures relating to giving: Exodus 34:26; 35:5–9; 36:5–7. What do you learn from them?

Compare the above Scriptures with Luke 6:38; Acts 4:32–37; 20:35; 2 Corinthians 8, 9:6–15; 1 Corinthians 16:1–3.

Differentiate between "paying tithes" and "gave themselves and all they had."

Support for God's work was commanded by God Himself, and it is taken seriously.

It was given before the law (Genesis 28:22).

It was commanded by God as a law (Leviticus 27:30–32).

Jesus advised against neglecting such orders (Matthew 23:23).

It was given to honor God and support the church (1 Corinthians 9:1–27).

How to Abound in the Grace of Giving

Giving should be done cheerfully, not grudgingly, with a heart of gratitude and a sense of urgency (Leviticus 22:29; 27:31).

My attitude toward the Lord, His church, and my assigned job in the kingdom (a recall to what He did for me at Calvary, the cleanup project on my life, and a general relationship He keeps with me) defines how deeply committed I am in the act of giving. Giving for God's work should be a part of every Christian's life. The grace to receive should match the grace to give. The Christian man or woman, having a vision of heaven and under the influence of the power of the Spirit, should not hold back. He gives freely for the work of the Lord.

Pay your tithes to the church where the truth is preached, where you are being fed with the Word of God regularly. There are licensed and registered churches with trained and ordained ministers who preach the gospel of our Lord Jesus Christ, under whose custodian every kingdom citizen aligns. To such, pay your tithes and give your free-will offerings according to the measure of your income.

Giving must be seen as an opportunity to give back to God. It is a holy sacrament (Psalm 20:1–9).

Remember, he who withholds corn [money], the people will curse … There is he who scatters and gives liberally and therefore tends toward prosperity, and there he who withholds and tends toward poverty. Give!

Benefits of Paying Tithes and Giving Offerings

Paying tithes provides evidence of your faith in God and establishes the joy of the abundance in the house of God. It courts divine blessings beyond your comprehension. God rebukes the devourer (Satan) because of you! You know that you belong to a family—the family of God.

An Evil Creeps into the Church

A preacher seizes the pulpit and declares he wants to make men rich. He tells how Jesus was never a poor man and stresses the need for all to become millionaires the next day. Many follow and bring in their seeds (money) to sow into preacher's life. A church is born.

He begins to build a castle and buys some expensive cars and airplanes with money contributed. His house is a choice piece and all we see is that "his God is not a poor God." Meanwhile, the poor and the less privileged go hungry and are deprived in that congregation. The elders cannot speak out because they have been bought with a piece of the cake.

Or a mega-church lays claim to a small, subservient local congregation, saying, "We own you. You took our name, and you must pay monetary remittances or tithes to us. Otherwise, we will use our connections and power to dissolve your congregation." Meanwhile, the local church is not established or groomed by the mega-church and is not supported in any way by it. Yet because membership is made up of a particular extraction, the local congregation must pay 10 percent or 20 percent or sometimes 100 percent of money collected to the mega-church. This happens in Europe, Asia, Canada, and the United States. The movement, named a church, deploys everybody to plant a church (without training or equipping). Once sent, the young church must send money to the mega. This is church gone commercial, without a defined business model. Something is fishy in this setting!

Differentiate among church denominations and their different modes of operations:

Pentecostals
Evangelicals
Baptists
Lutherans
Anglican Communion
Roman Catholics
Methodists
Apostolic faith
Seventh-day Adventist
Faith Tabernacle congregation
Presbyterians

Who manages your church money?

- Authorization of payments from church account
- Payments (writes and cuts the checks)
- Records (keeps the log of income and expense information)
- Provides the expense items in your church

If you must know, do the Math:

Add the stipend/salaries/wages for pastor or bishop or the laymen workers. Include the bills and other recurrent expenditure for the month. Add money spent for welfare and remittances.

Compare income from the finance department with calculated expenses from the two or more itemized expense reports. What do you find? Write down the difference here:

What do you think is wrong here?

What is good about the financial report you have just run?

Step up, meet your pastor or bishop, and share your thoughts.

The Need for Volunteer Workers
Action Needed!

In what capacity would you want to volunteer in church or fellowship for the next four to eight weeks?

Name
Date

Project Title
Details of job to be done

Estimated amount you saved for church
$........

The Role of Elders

> And in those days, when the number of the disciples was multiplied, there arose a murmuring of the Grecians against the Hebrews, because their widows were neglected in the daily ministration. Then the twelve called the multitude of the disciples unto them, and said, It is not reason that we should leave the word of God, and serve tables. Wherefore, brethren, look ye out among you seven men of honest report, full of the Holy Ghost and wisdom, whom we may appoint over this business. But we will give ourselves continually to prayer, and to the ministry of the word. And the saying pleased the whole multitude: and they chose Stephen, a man full of faith and of the Holy Ghost, and Philip, and Prochorus, and Nicanor, and Timon, and Parmenas, and Nicolas a proselyte of Antioch: Whom they set before the apostles: and when they had prayed, they laid their hands on them. And the word of God increased; and the number of the disciples multiplied in Jerusalem greatly; and a great company of the priests were obedient to the faith. (Acts 6:1–7)

Given that you are mature enough to decipher and render balanced judgment, what do you think is wrong with your system of operation in your church or fellowship? A few people are paying the bills and keep the Church running!

What solutions have you proffered to your pastor or bishop toward mitigating the problem?

Are you willing to be on the committee of elders from today?

Write your proposal and how things can improve. Be specific on processes, projects, and resources needed to execute the projects

Contact the leadership of your church or fellowship, They will call you, but meanwhile, go and pray for the Church.

Conclusion

If your money represents your time, strength, talents, and inheritance, then it is scriptural to allow God to control your money. The way we handle money shows the content of our true relationship with God (He gave His only Son), although Satan can use money or lack of it to separate us from God. A believer's attitude toward money should therefore be guided by integrity, generosity, and stewardship and not by selfishness and materialism.

Reflections

What drives you in the use of the money you have been given in life?

CHAPTER 18

Foundations

Revisit Your Foundations … Clean Them Up

"If the foundations be destroyed, what can the righteous do?"
(Psalm 11:3 KJV; 1 Peter 4:15–19 KJV).

> So everyone who hears these words of Mine and acts
> upon them [obeying them] will be like a sensible (prudent,
> practical, wise) man who built his house upon the rock.
> And the rain fell and the floods came and the winds blew
> and beat against that house; yet it did not fall, because it
> had been founded on the rock. And everyone who hears
> these words of Mine and does not do them will be like a
> stupid (foolish) man who built his house upon the sand.
> And the rain fell and the floods came and the winds blew
> and beat against that house, and it fell—and great and
> complete was the fall of it. (Matthew 7:24–27 AB)

The structure and longevity of a house is determined by, among other
factors, the strength of its foundation. According to Jesus' parable, a house
built on sandy soil is most likely to collapse when the winds and hurricanes
of this world begin to blow. To make sure that does not happen to us, He
advises that we hear His words, obey them, and lay a solid foundation.

Unfortunately, our generation is devoid of counsel and mentoring. Most people choose their ways of living and doing ministry. It is either their way or the highway ... and either of those usually leads them to destruction.

Foundations are important in life formations. They represent start-ups, engineered systems or processes that lead to solid structural establishments. If you make a wrong choice of a foundation structure, then you will find your house underwater when the flood comes. Make a concrete choice, and you will be secure.

Forming a Good Foundation from Birth

Moses was of the lineage of Levi. He was born when Israel was under the torture of their slave master, the Egyptians. It was natural for Moses and all the skilled men in Israel to take offense at the humiliation and massacre of Israelites. It was not out of place for him to recruit men of passion and valor to join in the crusade against injustice and hatred; more so he had good military training in the house of Pharaoh for some time. Though Moses was so close to God that God referred to him as a friend, he was, in fact, the meekest man on earth. Still, there was anger, especially when Israel marshaled a foray of complaints.

Jacob, at his death, remembered the orgy saga of his sons' anger against Shechem, son of Hamor, the Hivite, and the young men of Shechem (Genesis 34). He said, "Simeon and Levi are brethren; instruments of cruelty are in their habitations. O my soul, come not thou into their secret; unto their assembly, mine honor, be not thou united: for in their anger they slew a man, and in their self-will they dogged down a wall. Cursed be their anger, for it was fierce; and their wrath, for it was cruel: I will divide them in Jacob, and scatter them in Israel" (Genesis 49:5–7).

Anger was running in the blood of Levi and Simeon. That trait was there and formed a foundation that grew until the time Moses killed the Egyptian and continued into the wilderness, where the same anger made him strike the rock instead of speaking to the rock to get water for the people. Anger management could not solve this problem. It went off course, and Moses was denied entry into the Promised Land.

Pause a minute to remember that Moses was the meekest man on earth, spoke one-on-one with God, and was a very close friend of God's. We can say that Moses found favor in God's eyes. But it could have been worse, had he not developed these traits and testimonies.

Like many of us, the foundation of an evil nature (an Adam nature) resonates in us and speaks so loudly and proudly that men on the street can hardly decipher the natural birth from the new birth, even when we claim Jesus as Lord and Savior.

In our society and churches, we see many incidences of faulty foundations. Take the example of the new birth, where someone comes to Jesus Christ primarily because of the promises and the blessings in the package. This new convert has his eyes focused on the gift, as presented to him by the prosperity preacher. We know, however, that the central theme of the gospel of Jesus Christ is:

> *Christ died for our sins. He rose from the dead and was seen by many. All men will be resurrected and then come to judgment.*

The solid foundation of the truth of the gospel will produce quality Christians who will take the message of the good news beyond the horizon of church walls. At conversion, men should know that Christ died to save them from their sins, of which they were held bound and incapacitated. Jesus Christ came to the world (to live and die) so that He might devastate the power of sin in men's lives. The power to undo the grip of Satan on our souls is the primary purposes of Jesus' coming—to reconcile us back to God. The gospel sets men free from sin, self, and Satan.

"For the grace of God that bringeth salvation hath appeared to all men, teaching us that, denying ungodliness and worldly lusts, we should live soberly, righteously, and godly, in this present world; Looking for that blessed hope, and the glorious appearing of the great God and our Savior Jesus Christ; Who gave himself for us, that he might redeem us from all iniquity, and purify to himself a peculiar people, zealous of good works" (Titus 2:11–14 KJV).

The purpose for Jesus' coming to die for us was the foundation of the knowledge that sin debased man and got him out of the place of glory and favor and fellowship with God. Jesus needed to fix the disintegrated divine nature of man by His death on the cross; this, therefore, forms a basis for all living and engagement in ministry. The place of the cross in a life, career, or ministry sets a pace for the right foundation, without which engagements go the way of the world (though rebranded as representing Jesus Christ, they are a hybrid of the world system). Therefore, at birth there must be a conscious application of the death, the burial, and the resurrection of Jesus Christ and then the witnessing and the demonstration of the power and all doctrinal embellishments that dot the Christian faith.

"For the love of Christ constraints us; because we thus judge, that if one died for all, then were all dead: And that he died for all, that they which live should not henceforth live for themselves, but for him which died for them, and rose again. Wherefore henceforth know we no man after the flesh: yea, though we have known Christ after the flesh, yet now henceforth know we him no more. Therefore if any man be in Christ, he is a new creature: old things are passed away; behold, all things are become new" (2 Corinthians 5:14–17 KJV).

He died on the cross and all of us must come to the place of the cross and death. Jesus did not promise an easy passage through life, but He makes available grace and succor as we go through the narrow road of life. He enjoins all to look up to Him, just as the people looked up to the serpent figure that Moses held up in the wilderness.

Whatever the engagement is, we must come to the place of the cross and death to our wills, passions, and desires. Until then, we will not be perfectly fitted into God's kingdom processes. We must be consumed with the lesson of the cross and death of the Lord Jesus Christ. If we fail to inculcate this truth into us, we will struggle with sin, self, and Satan in life, career, and ministry. We should be able to say, without reservation, "I am crucified with Christ: nevertheless I live; yet not I, but Christ liveth in me: and the life which I now live in the flesh I live by the faith of the Son of God, who loved me, and gave himself for me" (Galatians 2:20 KJV).

When we do not fully understand the finished work of grace embedded in Jesus' death at Calvary, we tend to belittle grace and undermine the complete work of salvation. At new birth, Jesus paid it all. He paid for a faulty foundation, a curse that ancestral spirits bestowed on people. The knowledge of the complete work of grace is all we need to sail through the tortuous waters of life. At Calvary, God paid a ransom for our souls that the Devil stole away. We were enslaved and trapped by the forces of darkness, without a course or direction toward God. We were an enemy of God, but instead, Jesus Christ gave Himself up, died on the cross, and paid in full—a price for our souls.

The knowledge and import of this life of Christ is all that is needed to start a soul reengineering. This remodeling work of the soul and spirit of man gives him power and access to God. With this, the foundations of endemic sins and demonic influences and operations are bound and defeated.

There is, therefore, a glowing forth of the new life, a fragrance that begins to fill our world. When this happens, God would have planted a seed—His nature—in you. This new nature is the Spirit of God. He comes with a dislike of sin and a detachment from the grip of Satan. There is now no condemnation to those who are in Christ Jesus, those who walk not according to the whims of the flesh but to the promptings of the Spirit. In this new nature, with the seed of God (the Word of God) planted, the believer can be assured of security and peace, right at that moment and thereafter. Demons have no dwelling place in the believer and thus, the power that overcomes sin also overcomes Satan, because that power has gained control over the flesh and self.

At this point, fellowship with the Father is not drudgery; it is easy, and a free access is always there between this world and heaven. There is communication and friendship. There is liberty and a constant, sustainable relationship with God. All these are possible because Jesus came and died and rose again. These foundations must be taught and lived. Without them, we would have built our houses on a sandy soil, without grip or grit to stand on the day of test.

Get it All Together the Right Way (Life Applications)

You heard a voice telling you to go into ministry or become a pastor, to go for missions. You belong to a local church and have a job as a medical doctor or other lucrative career, and you are the breadwinner for your immediate and extended family. The urge is strong and the voice very clear. Your fiancée is not excited, however, and your parents think you are insane. Still, you must obey the call to fulfill this specific mandate. What do you do?

You need to be trained, tested, tried, and trusted and then entrusted with the lives of men, to fix lives, to engage in warfare, and to enlist with God for the program of heaven.

The Five T's of Spiritual Engagement

1. *Trained*

A primary need in the heart of God is to get training in a school. True, the Scriptures promise that the Holy Spirit will teach us all things, but any chosen vessel must be equipped with information, truth, and strategies on how to enlist in the armed forces of heaven. In 2 Corinthians 12:1–7 and Galatians 1:15–18, Paul tells us that after conversion (Acts 9), he went up to Arabia through Damascus and then back to Jerusalem, during which time he met those who guided him and instructed him in the things of God, though he had a good piece of legal training and exposure with Gamaliel. Lack of training in any engagement is a redefinition of "setting up for failure" at the beginning of the engagement. In the armed forces, soldiers are subjected to serious training before they are sent out to fight. In the Christian faith, naivety and ignorance have caused many to believe that training is a waste of time. No wonder those who are untrained find pleasure in misfiring at will, thereby killing fellow soldiers.

Leadership must insist on training to equip the church for the Great Commission. A trained soldier is a successful soldier. He knows what to do at any given time and how well to execute instructions from his commander. My advice: with all your getting, get wisdom; go for training.

2. *Tested*

God tests His children, more so one whom He must use. Testing is a necessary tool in His hands. The software that we use in information systems is subject to various tests before it is put into production: unit testing, user testing, environmental testing, integrated testing. The idea is to make sure that software products are without defect and devoid of bugs, because once in production, they are irretrievable.

Once an untrained pastor assumes his position, he fills his psyche with the notion that he is good enough to do anything and is beyond reproach. His flock places him on a pedestal, and that is the beginning of a big fall in the days of adversity. Usually, tests are not very pleasing to the flesh. Remember your examinations and tests as a student? It is tough to study all night. Your success depends heavily on your grade on the test, and because of this, you study for long hours.

In the school of life, tests are very important. God allows us, through testing times, to bring out the best in us and to qualify us for something bigger than we are used to. Like our professors, He uses tests to determine our placement and promotions. When God wants to use a man, He drills him. He tests the man.

When God Wants to Drill a Man

When God wants to drill a man,
And thrill a man,
And skill a man
When God wants to mold a man
To play the noblest part;
When He yearns with all His heart
To create so great and bold a man
That the entire world shall be amazed,
Watch His methods, watch His ways!
How He ruthlessly perfects
Whom He royally elects!
How He hammers him and hurts him,
And with mighty blows converts him
Into trial shapes of clay which
Only God understands;
While his tortured heart is crying
And he lifts beseeching hands!
How He bends but never breaks
When his good He undertakes;
How He uses whom He chooses,
And which every purpose fuses him;

By every act induces him
To try His splendor out—
God knows what He's about.

—Anonymous

3. Tried

At moments of advantage, when there is immediate gain and the preacher holds the ace, God is about to try him. This is not the same as testing. In testing, you are subjected to scrutiny, pressure, and hardship or hardness. When you are tried; it is a proof of character, an assessment of behavioral tendencies that may overrun you while in the field. The book of Job is handy here. In his prosperity, God allowed Satan to overrun Job. Satan devastated Job—his wife turned against him, his friends were a pain, and there was none on his side. Character and faith were on the line for Job.

With all that happened to Job, the gravest was not the loss of wealth and children; it was the silence of God. Between chapters two and thirty-eight, God was silent at Job, in the way the God was silent at Abraham (Genesis 16, 17) for thirteen years.

Normally, when your song begins to rhyme, the chords and keys begin to agree, the multitudes will gather. They begin a praise song and send congratulatory messages. Women and men are good at identifying with success. That may be the time of your trial—success! God wants to know what you will do with a little piece of success. Have you gone through the school of being weaned and tried under the fame and success story? Review how you got into the kingdom—how tears flowed at the sight of sin, how you behaved toward the opposite sex, how you treated and respected the clergy, how you revered God and holy things, how you behaved toward money entrusted to your care, how you seized power or members of your church from another preacher or church, and how you raised money, purporting that God asked you to do so … the list goes on. Have you been tried? Get back to God, and get it right before you continue.

4. Trusted

Trusted friends are rare, especially in our age of quick fixes and life on the fast lane. Trust is earned. God still searches for people He can trust. "And the Lord said unto Satan, Hast thou considered my servant Job, that there is none like him in the earth, a perfect and an upright man, one that feareth God, and escheweth evil?" (Job 1:8 KJV).

"And Moses said unto the children of Israel, See, the Lord hath called by name Bezaleel the son of Uri, the son of Hur, of the tribe of Judah; And he hath filled him with the spirit of God, in wisdom, in understanding, and in knowledge, and in all manner of workmanship; And to devise curious works, to work in gold, and in silver, and in brass, And in the cutting of stones, to set them, and in carving of wood, to make any manner of cunning work" (Exodus 35:30–33 KJV).

"And Bezaleel the son of Uri, the son of Hur, of the tribe of Judah, made all that the Lord commanded Moses" (Exodus 38:22 KJV).

God referred to Moses as His friend, "for I speak face to face with him." The depth of trust one has for another depends on the wealth of character of the one being trusted. While proof of your character may not be made known to admirers or even the opposition, it is imperative that the result of the proof comes clean, without blemish. Trust is one thing that cannot be bought with money or schemed through the pulpit. Men readily know those they can trust; God knows better.

In your quest to go places with the preaching of the gospel, one thing is important: a search for a life that can be trusted with the destiny of men. God is not in a hurry to parade a fleet of ill-equipped men on the warfront. I know He is still searching for men of character and will, men who can be trusted, and men who can keep the secrets of those who come to them. The search for men continues. Will God find you?

5. EnTrusted

The belief God places in a man to work with Him defies any reason. At your commissioning, a declaration goes forth for you to represent heaven. For me, this engagement is not to be taken lightly. It involves a mandate to be with Christ, to learn at His feet, to teach others the same message as taught by our forerunners, and to undo the schemes and plans of Satan in men's lives. This is a glorious undertaking.

As representatives of the kingdom, God wants us to engage in the effort of rescuing people from the grip of evil and leading them to God, as they discover a new way of living in Jesus Christ. This belief that God has placed in us positions us to continue with the defense of the truth as the early church fathers did.

Paul, at the very end of his ministry, with martyrdom stirring before him, dictated a letter for his spiritual son, Timothy. Paul encouraged Timothy to hold on to what he had been taught, to guard and lead believers away from heresies and error, to stand firm against temptations, and to persevere through trials and pass on the good news to generations to come. The same charge goes out to us today. Here's what Paul told Timothy:

"You therefore, my son, be strong in the grace that is in Christ Jesus. The things which you have heard from me in the presence of many witnesses, entrust these to faithful men who will be able to teach others also" (2 Timothy 2:12).

We find similar analogy in Ezra and Nehemiah. Both were committed to rebuilding the walls of Jerusalem and teaching God's truth in the land. The walls needed rebuilding, and so did the lives of men in the temple and in the pews, so Ezra, the scribe, committed to learning and teaching and doing the Word of God. There was a learning and then the teaching and an effective demonstration of the Word he taught. And thus it was passed on to younger generations, to men of honor. We are called to the same ministry of learning, teaching, and doing the Word of God.

Discover the Five P's of the Execution Process

To help you align with God's will, start by asking these basic questions: Why am I in the world? What is God's plan for me? What exactly is my role in the overall plan? How can I achieve what God has in store for me? Very few people get answers to these questions immediately.

You may use this format to get started. God's calling must be accompanied by the following "Five P's." Discover your Five P's and guard them carefully.

1. *Purpose:* This is the lifeline and specific ministry into which you are called. Check the fivefold ministries in Ephesians.4:11–13 and Galatians 1:1–3. Make sure you know God is calling. Do not jump into it.

2. *Plan:* Get your strategies right with the Holy Spirit as your chief operating officer. Itemize your settings, your structures, and your strategies. Develop a case for your being and your calling. What is it that you intend to add to the value for which heaven is looking? *What value are you bringing on to the table?* Differentiate your offering and stand out with a mission!

3. *Platform:* This is the place where you choose to deliver your message. This can be a church, an organization, a music band, or a ministry that offers itself as a channel or a denomination to express your calling. Where is your pulpit? In what concentration area may we look for you? Is it at the church, outer missions without walls, in organized groups, institutions, mental health facilities, prisons, or hospitals? These are area of operation; your environment, your catchment niche. Find out what your area is.

4. *People:* Who are your audience? To which target groups are you reaching out? This information will help in designing your plan.

5. *Pipes and conduits:* What are your channels of distribution? What materials do you need for the project? What skill sets and training do you have or need to ensure fruitful results and that the ultimate desire of heaven is met. With whom are you likely to collaborate and partner?

Ministry and any other form of engagement require constant review and evaluation, as there may be a diminishing marginality in expected output. Output here is not limited to tangible, physical gains but tends to include faithfulness, saved souls, increase in the knowledge of the Word of God and changed lives for Jesus.

Review, Restock, Restrategize, Relaunch ... Rebounce

In all circumstances, an overall goal is to add value and bring a change in how things are done. When there is a red flag in ministry operations or vision, the tendency usually is to call it quits; Or sometimes the Monday blues come upon the man of God, when a review of Sunday's sermon does not seem to fit or when results and strategies look rusty or mundane. Your once-vibrant calling seems clogged and the very fabric of your unbending resolve to serve the Lord, who saved you with a mighty and strong hand, is eaten up. At such moments, you are nose-diving into pity and self-defeat. A sense of "it's all over" heavily weighs on you. Here, an economist would say your marginal productivity is negative.

It is not over yet. Yes, you may have fallen short, but you are not short of the grace and mercy of God. David said, "Though I fall seven times, yet will I rise again."

Here again is my offer:

1. *Review your actions and projects.* Be careful that you are not misquoting God. Check your last call in prayer, studious search of the Word of God, and witnessing about His goodness or even what's been revealed.

2. *Restrategize: revisit Bethel.* This is the house of God. Discover whether the trend you used is still in vogue in today's technology-driven world. Always review and check your original design, your masterpiece from God, as it was delivered to you from the beginning—that original prototype from God upon which every other thing has been built. Check to see if Jesus Christ is being magnified and worshipped. He is the hub in the wheel. Be sure that God is the central point of focus, not you or the air of importance that has blown your way by reason of exploits and advantages. Remember that the Holy Spirit is a gentle personality. Do you still honor Him?

3. *Now you can begin some asset mapping.* Begin by rebranding, and employ the strategy of adding values and flavor to what you used to do. Get more training and review your five P's. Find out new lifestyles of your people, along with their needs and preferences. Match that with what God wants to fix in their lives, with what the need is (these are their core needs and value preferences). Anything outside the needs of the people (example: dealing with sin and seeking revival) would reduce ministry to merely an ordinary project. If ministry does not meet people at their points of spiritually caring, there might be negative marginal productivity.

4. *Realign the pipe and the conduit.* It could be a switch to high tech or a new strategy of using technology to meet a wider reach (example: witnessing and mentoring using Facebook or Twitter). The trick here is to use the right tool at the right time, to understand the trend with people and their preferences

5. *Reengineering for spiritual stimuli.* Most times, a clog on the wheel may arise from spiritual oppositions and combatant operations in the realm of the spirit. Some issues do not go away except by fasting and prayer—albeit some serious intercessory prayers—so there is need to engage in spiritual warfare for the work to move smoothly (Nehemiah 1, 2, 3).

Spiritual solutions are received on the altar of prayer. There is need to "PUSH" (Pray Until Something Happens) for the enemy of our souls to be brought under our feet. One of our assigned duties as priests is to pronounce judgment on satanic operations in our homes, society, and ministry. Such influence should not be tolerated in any way.

CHAPTER 19

Course Review

Take-away: Homework

1. *Understanding the New Birth*
   - What are the things people usually assume could make them qualify to be Christians but that cannot? Read Acts 10.
   - Narrate briefly your personal experience of the New Birth.
   - You would have heard about the gospel of our Lord Jesus Christ before the day you finally surrendered to Him. Enumerate the factors that didn't allow you to give your life the first time someone preached to you.
   - Now that you are born again, what have you enjoyed as a Christian that you never experienced before?

2. *Repentance from Dead Works*
   - If for any reason temptation leads you to sin, what should be your attitude at that moment when you realize that you just sinned as a child of God? 1John 1

3. *Discovering Your New Self*
   - What is your relationship with God now that you are new, and how does God see you?
   - How do you relate with your old pals and yet-to-be-saved relations?

- What are the major differences between you and your unsaved friends? (1 Peter 2).

4. *Bible, Trinity, and Devil*
   - Write down the order in which the books of the Bible appear and their abbreviations.
   - How biblical is the reading of the Psalms as the only book of the Bible?

5. *Quiet Time*
   - Your teacher will suggest a chapter of the Bible to read. Read until something strikes you, and then mediate on it. Write down the thought that comes to you. Rediscover two or three different points that strike you from searching the Scriptures with your study Bible.
   - Write a very short prayer on any of these types of prayers following the guideline we have in the Lord's Prayer: adoration, confession, thanksgiving, supplication/petition.

6. *Baptism*
   - Does baptism wash away your sins in the water? Discuss.
   - To speak in tongues is a demonstration that you have "arrived" as a Christian. Yes or no? Write down at least five points on speaking in tongues as recorded in 1 Corinthians 14.

7. *Personal Evangelism*
   - Write all the modes we can use for personal evangelism.
   - The Bible says we are the epistle of the Most High God (2 Corinthians 3:2). How can this Scripture affect our personal evangelism, overtly and covertly?

8. *Christian Conduct*
   - Discuss briefly what this phrase means: "unsaintly saints." Make use of the points from our study on Christian conduct.
   - The Bible enjoins us to be at peace with all men. How do we handle the people who always get on our nerves? Quote Scriptures to support your answer.

9. *Christian Discipline*
   • "All good and perfect gifts are from God Almighty." How can we relate this to the injunction on the moderation in all things in Philippians 4:5?

10. *Fasting and Prayer*
    • Name three people in the Bible who fasted. Why do you think they did so?
    • What spiritual advantages do you enjoy from fasting?
      Fasting should be a habit that the Christian cultivates. Start today.

11. *Divine Healing*
    • The Bible says that healing is the children's meat (Matthew 15:28). Is it scriptural to seek medical attention at the onset of every sickness? (Exodus 15:26; Psalm 127:1; 103:3).
    • Enumerate the sources of illness as discussed in this book. From which one of them does your illness normally come? Align your confessions with what the Bible says about you (Joshua 1:8; 1 Peter 2:24).

12. *Restitution, Holy Marriage, and Tithe*
    • Restitution may be difficult, but it is important to clear your mind of obstacles to heaven. In the presence of the Holy Spirit, ask God to give you the grace to begin restitution today.
    • How does Proverbs 3:9a describe our giving to God? Write it down, and tell God that this is what you intend to do.

13. *Deliverance*
    • How many possible demonic covenants could be made by one single visit to a native doctor?
    • Name four Christian "cults." What are the likely problems of becoming a member of any of them?

14. *Second Coming of Christ*
    • What do you know about the rapture (that is, the second coming of Jesus Christ)? Do you believe in it? Use Bible quotations for support.

- It is appointed unto man to die once after that judgment. Discuss with Bible references.

15. *Millennial Reign and Coming Judgment*
- "I'd rather be a doorkeeper in the house of God" (Psalm 84:10). Discuss this passage and write the lesson learned from your findings.
- What rewards await a successful believer when he gets to heaven? (Daniel 12:3).

Reflections

CHAPTER 20

Final Words

So when they had come together, they asked him, "Lord, will you at this time restore the kingdom to Israel?" He said to them, "It is not for you to know times or seasons that the Father has fixed by his own authority. But you will receive power when the Holy Spirit has come upon you, and you will be my witnesses in Jerusalem and in all Judea and Samaria, and to the end of the earth." And when he had said these things, as they were looking on, he was lifted up, and a cloud took him out of their sight. And while they were gazing into heaven as he went, behold, two men stood by them in white robes, and said, "Men of Galilee, why do you stand looking into heaven? This Jesus, who was taken up from you into heaven, will come in the same way as you saw him go into heaven." (Acts 1:6–11)

An Undeniable Truth

You are in your car driving home. Thoughts wander to the game you want to see or the meal you want to eat, when suddenly, a sound unlike any you've ever heard fills the air. The sound is high above you. Is it a trumpet? A choir? A choir of trumpets? You don't know, but you want to know. So you pull over, get out of your car, and look up. As you do, you see you aren't the only curious one. The roadside has become a parking lot. Car doors are open, and people are staring at the sky. Shoppers are racing out of the grocery store. The Little League baseball game across the street has come to a halt. Players and parents are searching the clouds. And what they see—and what you see—has never been seen.

It's as if the skies are a curtain, and the drapes of the atmosphere part. A brilliant light streams down to earth, but there are no shadows. Riding on the stream of light is an endless fleet of angels. They pass through the curtains until they occupy every square inch of the sky. Thousands of silvery wings rise and fall in unison, and over the sound of the trumpets, you can hear the cherubim and seraphim chanting, "Holy, holy, holy." The final flank of angels is followed by twenty-four silver-bearded elders and a multitude of souls who join the angels in worship.

Presently, the movement stops, and the trumpets are silent, leaving only the triumphant triplet: holy, holy, holy. Between each word is a pause, a profound reverence. You hear your voice join in the chorus. You don't know why you say the words, but you know you must. Suddenly, the heavens are quiet. All is quiet. The angels turn, you turn, the entire world turns—and there He is: Jesus. Through waves of light you see the silhouetted figure of Christ the King. He is on top of a great stallion, and the stallion is on top of a billowing cloud. He opens his mouth, and you are surrounded by his declaration: "I am the Alpha and the Omega."

The angels bow their heads. The elders remove their crowns. Before you is a figure so consuming that you know—instantly, you know: Nothing else matters. You forget stock markets and school reports. Sales meetings and football games come to an end. Nothing is newsworthy. All that mattered, matter no more … for Christ has come.

As we journey toward eternity, it becomes imperative for each one of us to make a conscious effort to eliminate every weight and sin that beset us so that we can run the race God has set before us with patience. There are many Christians who started off yesterday but who have allowed these weights to prevent them from making meaningful progress or who are in a different race entirely. Thank God for those who are still in the race.

It is for this reason that I plead for an honest self-appraisal of your life. Give quality attention to the following questions:

Are there sins on which you do not want to preach?

> Are there sins you are always ready to excuse because you consider them small or because you have "better" names for them?
>
> Are there sins you prefer to commit when no one is around?
>
> Are there sins that readily hold you captive?
>
> Are there sins that always seem to stand in your way when you really feel like talking with God?
>
> Are there sins you continually try to make yourself believe are a weakness, arising from the peculiarity of your tribe, family profession, or environment?
>
> Remember, the Devil may provide pleasures and benefits of sins, but he will always hide the price tag that eternal punishment offers.
>
> Confess all known sins today, and rededicate your life to the soon-coming King, Jesus Christ. May God not allow any sin to stand in your way to heaven. Amen.

Some Clips from Isolated Studies
The Power of His Resurrection

At the turn of the page, history recognizes that a divine personality changed the course of events and reordered the timing of all human schemes, sciences, and thoughts. In Him, all things consist and are carved out or formed. He is the hub and the center, the fulcrum for every joint. All things were made by and for Him, the embodiment of life and expectation of the dead and the living. A dial to His name causes panic—nay, a tsunami—turmoil, and a devastating earthquake among demons in hell. Suffice to say that the power and authority in this personality brings hope, encouragement, healing, energized vigor, and sustainable strength to the weak. He is Jesus Christ; the only and same man who conquered death and has an empty tomb to show for it. Beyond philosophy and semantics, Jesus has proved to be the only name God has given men to find salvation. He comes to bear on humanity with certain power and authority to affect life.

The free "download" is easy and without interference. It comes in a bundle: full health-care plan without deductibles, upfront fully paid for 401(k), kids' education, housing, and vacations. The password for this download is *faith* in Jesus. It's that simple.

I can hear you say, "There is a price more than meets the eye, for nothing is free." Remember, this is not a business school class where we calculate the cost of free stuff. The price was paid long before this age, paid at the cross of Calvary. The title deed was obtained on the resurrection, the transaction for the emancipation for your soul. The receipt obtained, an empty grave, was completed, packaged, and now ready for delivery. All these are possible as a result of Jesus' resurrection from the grave.

Suffice to say that there is a *power* that raised Him. It is the power of the Holy Spirit (Ephesians 1:15–21). The death and resurrection of Jesus Christ would be theoretical if the power and authority that comes with it was not made to bear on the people of faith. In other words, Jesus is not risen (especially in your life) if the Devil still plays a game with you. Jesus is not risen if the Devil still dominates and rules your thoughts and organizes evil schemes and projects for you, your involvement in church activities notwithstanding. The Devil can ebb out your life without your knowing.

The price paid at Calvary is a waste if you are not demonstrating the power of His resurrection in your home, in your office, in your church, on the streets, and in the malls. This power that raised Him up from the grave is the Holy Spirit (Acts 1:8), and I ask you: Have you received the baptism of the Holy Spirit? Do you still experience demonic oppression? Is your soul (emotion, mind, and personality) jinxed? Are you under the influence of certain unknown powers, enslaved to their whims and caprice? There is help for you. Come for a download—a free download from the throne of God.

This is Passover time, when at least one prisoner must be set free. That power that raised Jesus up will lift you up as well. Call in, and come straight in. We'll match power with power! You will be free, completely!

Arise, Your Light Has Come!
An Easter Story

On January 3, 2007, Wesley Autrey, a fifty-year-old African American construction worker and US navy veteran, was waiting for the local train at the 137th Street and Broadway in Manhattan around 12:45 p.m. He was taking his two daughters, Syshe, age four, and Shuqui, age six, home before work. Nearby, a twenty-year-old man, later identified as Cameron Hollopeter, started having convulsions from a seizure disorder, collapsed, and fell to the tracks between the two rails. The headlights of the No. 1 train suddenly appeared, heading toward them.

According to the *New York Times*, while other bystanders watched in horror at the inevitable impending death of this unfortunate young man, Wesley Autrey quickly jumped onto the tracks, placed his body on top of the convulsing young man, and pressed him down in a space roughly a foot deep. The train brakes screeched, but it could not stop before running over the top of the men. Autrey sustained some bruises, but both men survived.

The story reminds me of the statement that Jesus Christ made to His disciples in John 15:13—"Greater love hath no man than this that a man would lay down his life for his friends." The Bible also states that while we were yet sinners, Christ died for our sins. While we were strangers to him, He laid down his life for us. The Easter message transcends the miracle of a man who died and rose again after three days. The glory of the event is the millions of people who experience life today because of the death of one man.

While Jesus hung on the cross, He persisted through the pain, the rejection, and the disgrace because His thoughts were filled with the millions who would live because He paid the price for their punishment. Besides the freedom from the penalty of sin, His death also provided freedom from the power of sin to as many as receive this precious gift. Indeed, His body was broken to set us free from the power of sin, and His blood was shed to free us from the penalty of sin. Romans 6:23 reads, "The wages of sin is death, but the gift of God is eternal life."

Jesus Christ died because He bore our sins and had to pay the price for them. If He did not rise from the dead, we would still be bound by sin today, hopeless and awaiting God's judgment, but His resurrection, which

211

we celebrate every Easter season, is a symbol of the new life we have been given in Christ, free from the penalty and power of sin. When He died, we died with Him, and the wages of sin were paid for. As we live each day through Christ, we are forever declared, not guilty as we live a new life in the spirit.

This is the grace of God. According to Titus 2:11, "The grace of God that brings salvation has been revealed to all men. It teaches us to say no to sin and ungodliness." What an amazing victory and liberation! We no longer have to struggle with sin or give in helplessly to the desires of the flesh. As we celebrate the Easter season, I pray that we review the glorious significance of the events. I pray it would be an opportunity to meditate on God's Word and take hold of the victory that has been given to us. We can live beyond sinful habits, desires, and lifestyles that plagued us in our ignorance. We can say no to sin and trust God every day for strength to overcome. He who began a good work in you is faithful to complete it.

Reflections

CHAPTER 21

Share the Fun, the Burden, and the Expectations

Sometime in 1984, the Lord, through the leadership of His church, appointed me to lead the Counseling Committee in the Christian Union. That was the start of my ministry. Through the years, I have observed young and old in ministry, especially my mentors (Charles Achonwa, Gbile Akanni, Chris Okeke, et al), and realize that God used men to get me to where I am today.

I am grateful to all my mentors. I owe the Lord my life and times on earth, to serve and gratefully yield to His tutoring and instructions. I have been to places (missions fields in Malawi, Kenya, Israel, Mozambique, and South Africa) and have seen the big, the great, and the mighty with affluent air; some, abased to grass. I have also been encouraged to observe men of valor wade through Satan's den, unabated, winning and ready to win again the battle of life and ministry. By their experience and the Word of God spoken to my heart, I am encouraged to continue to fight to win.

I want to conclude this book with a few words of encouragement to you. Whether in ministry or in life, there is a path we must all tread and be assured of one thing: that the Lord's "well done" awaits us on the other side of the divide. As the times pass, the end will come sooner than we think. Ministry or professionalism will draw its curtains. A day will come when every man's work will come to judgment and will be exposed, to be tested by fire, a day of accountability. I encourage you to take life at its best. Seize every opportunity to observe to do His will, according to Scriptures. Engage in works that profit heaven and eternity. Indulge in divine projects. Eschew evil and shun wickedness, bickering, and lies. Be holy, for your heavenly Father is holy. Tread softly with the orphan and the widow. Handle them with care because their cry to their heavenly Father will never go unheard and unanswered.

Remember the day of accountability and shun evil! God will bring all works in the open and will judge every man according to the works done in the flesh.

By way of preparing for the day of the Lord, I introduce some heavenly projects—projects that cut deep into the heart of God. They were given to affect the lives of men and women on earth, the type you find in Matthew 25. As the urge to do the Lord's work lurks in my heart, the wherewithal to execute these projects is relevant to the passion.

Arising from such scarce resource, I went to fetch wood; I went fishing. Truly, the vision is clear, and the passion is stronger than when it was received. Now, I encourage you to join the train of divine projects with me.

It was not easy combining missionary engagement with managing offshore textile business operations for Derry Robinson & Company (a UK firm) in Africa, after a three-year stint in the financial investment industry and editing scripts in a business journal publishing house. That was exactly my preoccupation for twelve years (1990–2002). I rose from customer service representative to a manager and then to African representative in Ghana, Cotonou, and Malawi, respectively. The passion for the poor African rural dwellers fueled my drive to enroll in the Redeemers Bible College. and then I engaged in preaching and pastoring at the same time. HIV/AIDS rehabilitation and economic empowerment projects across the east and southern African regions were, among other engagements and platforms, what I used to vent my passion (thanks to the proceeds from the business operations).

Starvation, deaths as a result of poor medical administration and general impoverishment that I lived with are stories that I would not want to replay in this book. Lives were saved, but many were snuffed through to eternity. Through it all, I managed life with a miserable reconciliation. I vowed to help poor Africans in the best possible way. I worked with the church on one hand (without pay or support) and Derry Robinson & Company on the other hand (with a handsome return on investment). Then I moved to the United States in February 2002.

RCCG Dominion Center was established as a not-for-profit group in the state of Ohio in January 2003. The church started off in Mason Cincinnati, Ohio, in August 2002. As we determined to accomplish the mandate God gave us, we hopped from the Hampton Inn, Englewood, to Chimney Oaks Club House and then to the Presbyterian church break room, all located in Dayton, Ohio. We held worship services in Avondale Community Center (Hirsch Center) on Reading Road, Cincinnati, Ohio, and then moved to Courtyard by Marriott Hotel in Blue Ash before we found office space on Northland Boulevard in Springdale, Ohio. When the office space proved very small for us, we moved again to the YMCA in Fairfield, Cincinnati.

It was in Fairfield, Ohio, that God visited us and provided the massive facility we renamed a city. There were times when we held worship in the open field when we were locked out of our rented places of worship. Our story is to let you know the faithfulness of God. May I ask, Are you believing God for a place of worship? Does the work of the kingdom scare you, and there seems to be no escape route for you? Listen, God will execute His work. Though the vision tarries, wait for it, for the vision is for an appointed time. It may delay. Please wait for it!

An Exhilarating Time … June 9, 2009

We bid for one of the Cincinnati Public School facilities. Before the auction, the church was ready to make a down payment of a certain sum for a midsize facility on the sweet side of town. That got pitched by some act of God. As we walked onto the floor, we had a conviction that should our best be nixed by some deep pockets, like Dress Homes, Fischer Homes, Inverness Homes, or other investors, we would go home with pride. After all, we had done our best.

Behold, the tale turned sweet—our bid won the day. Whatever happened to the deep pockets that faithful day was a mystery yet to be unraveled. We bought the facility for less than the amount we budgeted for a down payment. We paid cash within a very short wait time. There was no loan processing. No mortgage payment. The transaction was akin to new birth—quick and concise, fully paid for by God through some faithful friends and brethren.

Come, Join This Train …

> "For every one that useth milk is unskillful the word of righteousness for he is a babe; But strong meat belongeth to them that that are of full age, even those who by reason of use have their senses exercised to discern both good and evil" (Hebrews 5:13–14).

Spiritual maturity comes by use of God's gifts, the expression of the inner buildup of character, devotion, and application (by reason of use) of learned traits. This means getting your hands dirty, doing the work in ministry. These are days of doing the work, not talking the talk. The key words are *by reason of use*, and they do not come by mere wishes. The application comes by getting involved in the vineyard, by doing something that positively affects people in time and eternity.

I want to encourage you to fill a gap in the community or your local church and be useful. Get your hands dirty and your purse deflated by way of investing in heavenly projects. To sit and watch projects executed in the church and think that it is an exclusive preserve of ordained men of God or a must-do for other folks is an aberration of the kingdom principle. As a child of the kingdom, you are a part of what we do. Do not alienate yourself from the kingdom, taking the posture of a stranger in the household of faith.

The work should involve every member of a local congregation. Everyone must strive to excel in the area of his calling, and everyone should be marked present on heaven's register.

The training you have received in this book will be most beneficial if it is applied to daily ministerial life by way of use and doing. And this is the whole essence of my testimony of how God started with me in the United States. It is to give you hope and a purpose toward hashing out a ministry. It is to help you align with God and subsequently to join our train in ministry, wherever and whatever your local church domain may be. Be open to God's choice to find use in the ten departments of ministry in which He has asked to use you as a channel to satisfy the needs of people in your community.

I believe you are a great tool in the hands of the Lord in these last days before the closure process of this earthly engagement. The Lord demands that we employ our resources toward things that have eternal value, which is to use our earthly materials and funds (via these projects) on people, to the end that the people may know Jesus Christ and be discipled; to be like Him. Second is to create in man the essence of living, the very purpose for his creation, and thereby curb homicides and associated criminal acts. Third is to affect our communities, government, and the professional institutions with ethical values that point to better ways of doing business. These we want to accomplish with your participation and investment.

Here's a synopsis of the departments in our portfolio:

1. Dominion Health

Vision
To meet the health needs of every man we meet (spirit, soul, and body).

Mission Statement and Values
A specialized unit of the RCCG, Dominion Center, set up to meet the health needs of the community and the world. Locally, the unit achieves its objectives through the provision of clinical services and public health education. Globally, Dominion Health extends its reaches to developing countries through securing donations of used medical equipment in good working condition from area hospitals and shipping them to developing countries for use in hospitals and health care facilities, where this equipment is not readily available or easily accessible. In the same vein, nonperishable medical supplies are obtained and shared with those who desperately need but cannot afford them in hospitals and health care facilities in developing countries.

Program Initiatives
- Community-based clinic
- Health education program
- Technology-sharing program
- Medical supplies program
- Medical missions

Community-Based Clinic

This is a stand-alone outpatient clinic that provides free primary medical services to individuals and families living in the local community. It is staffed by medical and other health care professionals who are registered to practice in the state and choose to volunteer their services.

Health Education Program

This is a program that collates information and puts it all together in a consumer-friendly manner for the general public and school children to encourage behavioral change to lifestyles that promote healthy living. Printed materials address common communicable and no communicable diseases and how they can be avoided. In addition, information includes screening tools and accessible resources to treat or mitigate the effects of the conditions and prevent complications if detected at screening.

Technology-Sharing Program

This is a program that receives donations of used but functioning medical equipment, which hospitals and health care facilities want to get rid of as they upgrade their medical equipment. Such equipment is checked and repaired by biomedical engineering firms and consultants to ensure that it is in working order. It is then shipped to their mission bases. There is no cost or obligation attached to this effort.

2. Dominion Technologies (Computer Training Program)

This is a retooling service geared toward providing a lifeline effort, focused on benchmarking, leveraging, and giving a head start in technology and process-solution improvements. It's a community outreach that is people-oriented. Our passion is to get you back to work

Scope of Training (Starter Program)
- Basic computing
- Induction to Microsoft certified systems
- Telecommunication systems
- Financial modules and applications

Objectives
1. To get high school freshmen and seniors a head start in IT tool kit and supporting portfolios
2. To use professionals in our product delivery so that skills and tool kits used in industry are an everyday life experience
3. To facilitate a one-time certification (examination) engagement
4. To put in place an operable and sustainable job placement strategy
5. To pass on a family legacy of uninterrupted skilled development and process improvement in our community

3. Library

We hope to develop a digital library and web-based content that will house Gen-X value-added information. Music Hall of Fame and Recording Cave will serve our community in learning and practice of the art of music. Such content like the Afro beats, reggae, and classics are not-too-common styles among the Christian community. We intend to understudy, practice, and perform such shows using talented but spirit-filled folks for the upcoming generation.

4. Community Center (Day Care, Community Learning Center)
   The Kingdom Kids Day Care is an outreach arm of the church

5. Missions and School of Ministry (Dominion College) Modular Schedule

Objectives of School of Ministry

1. To equip the saints with the knowledge, power, and lifestyle in daily following, serving, and demonstrating the power of God through Jesus Christ

2. To educate, inform, and be involved with the work of the Master through our local churches and other ministries in the entire body of Christ

3. To affect the church, society, communities, and individual lives with the gospel of our Lord Jesus Christ in a practical, positive, and personal way, using tool kits of professionalism on one hand and ministry on the other

Special Classes

1. School of Disciples—a radical, different kind of living and ministering, driven by "What would Jesus do in my situation and circumstance?"

The school is exactly what it says it is: a "school" where we come to study, think, and pray on what it means to live the Christian life; the Jesus way. It is following Jesus, as individuals and together, as members of Christ's body, the church. It is a difficult calling, and we can only fully pursue this call if we are biblically grounded and theologically informed.

We are poised to reinvigorate lost synergies and a hunger for righteousness in both church and society, and thus our passion and conviction is to infuse humanity with the "infectious disease of radical change." The church is in constant need of renewed worship and testimony—the determined struggle of faith seeking understanding. The School of Discipleship is a place of reconceiving what it means to follow Jesus. It is a time of reorientation, a place where each of us gathers for reflection and renewal at the altar (call it revival) to respond to the imperatives of Christ's kingdom today, as we respond to the call to follow along the pilgrims' journey. Other specialty classes are:

- ➤ Tent-Making Ministry
- ➤ Christian Ministry in a Digital Age
- ➤ African Missions and Cultural Integration
- ➤ Ministering to Immigrants

Core College Courses of School of Ministry include but are not limited to those listed below:

Session A		Session B	
Week 1	Pastor as Interpreter of the Bible	Week 11	The Kingdom: Principles & Practice (Rule of Law, Governance, Mandate)
Week 2	Pastoral Care for Spiritual Formation	Week 12	Pastoral Leadership and Administration
Week 3	Theological Heritage I (Prayer)	Week 13	Formation for Christian Discipleship
Week 4	Practice of Preaching	Week 14	Homiletics
Week 5	Our Mission from God: Evangelism	Week 15	Pastoral Care and Counseling
Week 6	Theological Heritage II (Word)	Week 16	The Ministry of the Holy Spirit
Week 7	Worship and Sacraments	Week 17	Apologetics
Week 8	Pentecostal Movement	Week 18	The Church & the State
Week 9	Eschatology	Week 19	Angels & Demons
Week 10	Contemporary Theology	Week 20	Theology and Practice of Ministry (Ethics)

Other Ministry Projects Under Construction
Food pantry
Music studio
Youth after-school center
Business incubator (entrepreneurial empowerment)
Media and publications

Thanks for Investing!

You have gone through the training of the study book, *Digging for Gold*. You have also seen our projects. The Lord's instruction to us is that we should recruit faithful men and women into this assigned job to cooperatively join hands with us in executing the project. The truth is that time is not on our side. The need to complete the project and continue with the work of soul winning is central in our plan. Our calling is "to present every man perfect in Christ."

It is my sincere prayer that the Lord will find you and begin the good work He promised to accomplish by your hands here in Dominion Center, Cincinnati, Ohio, and other parts of our mission outreaches in Africa. Remember, you are God's battle ax, sharp and studded with grace, ready to pull down and destroy the kingdom of darkness and rebuild the broken walls of Jerusalem. We intend to build lives, reconstruct wasting synergies, and preach and disciple men and women for the Lord Jesus Christ. Let's sing my song together:

We are God's battle axe
We are God's battle axe
We are God's battle axe
We are God's battle axe, pulling down walls of darkness
Raising the banner of Jesus high
We are God's battle axe, saving the souls of men
Presenting every man perfect in Christ

I count on you, as the Lord requests of you, to employ your resources in the work of the kingdom. The time is running out; we do not have the leisure of engaging in frivolities nor being involved in things that do not affect heaven and eternity. We are called to serve, to save the lost. I encourage you to get in the game and be involved. The Lord is waiting, and we are waiting on you too. Before the flight, let's get busy. Let's be found of Him, occupying and engaged in the kingdom's business of soul winning, for He will surely come back.

"For the Lord Himself shall descend from heaven with a shout, with the voice of the archangel, and with the trump of God, and the dead in Christ shall rise first; Then we which are alive and remain shall be caught up together with them in the clouds, to meet the Lord in the air and so shall we ever be with the Lord. Therefore comfort one another with these words" (Thessalonians 4:16–18).

Come, join this train of investors in the vineyard of God. The return on investment is huge. We know that, and there is an assurance that heaven is keeping records. Your labor will not be in vain. Our God will bless you abundantly.

"Therefore, my beloved brethren, be ye steadfast, unmovable, always abounding in the work of the Lord, forasmuch as ye know that your labor of love is not in vain in the Lord" (1 Corinthians 15:58).

Keep the faith and be strong in the power of His might. Fight the good fight of faith, and please always remain fervent for the Lord Jesus in life and in ministry. Keep it simple. Thanks for your time. Pray for me, please.
Emmanuel Elendu
Email: emmaelendu@yahoo.com

REFERENCES

1. Achonwa, Charles. Unpublished Sermon Notes (Lagos, Nigeria: Doulos Ministries, 1984).
2. Akanni, Gbile. Unpublished Sermon Notes (Gboko, Nigeria: Peace House, 1999).
3. Alcorn, Randy. *The Grace and Truth Paradox* (Eternity Perspective Ministries, Teaching Notes, 2012).
4. Anonymous. "When God Drill a Man."
5. Corelli, Marie. *The Sorrows of Satan* (Oxford, UK: Oxford University Press, 1895).
6. Elendu, Emmanuel. Unpublished Sermon Notes at RCCG Dominion Center, Cincinnati & Dayton Ohio, 2002 through 2014.
7. Lifelines Publications. Unpublished monthly magazines of RCCG, Dominion Center, Cincinnati. Ohio (various articles, 2010 through 2014).
8. Nweke, Dr. Ferdinand. *Understanding Life* (Cincinnati, Ohio: Truth Institute of Eternity Ministries, 2013).
9. Okeke, Chris. Unpublished Sermon Notes (Nigeria: Scripture Union 1996).
10. Redeemed Christian Church of God. Unpublished Believers Class Manual (Training).
11. Walters, Ron. "Aging & Living Your Full Potentials," 2013. (Provided by Ron Walters, Sr. VP Ministry Relations, Salem Communications).

Other Books by Emmanuel Elendu
1. *Personal Discipleship*
2. *Before You Quit*
3. *Anatomy of the Virgin Birth*
4. *He Got Me Jazzed & Inspired*